Nancy Welch's

4

INGREDIENT

Cookbook

Nancy Welch's
4 INGREDIENT Cookbook

It has been ten years since I printed my last cookbook, *Cooking on the Go*. At that time, I had two small sons, a husband and a fulltime job hosting a daily television show for women. In the introduction of that book, I said that my cooking had to have short cuts and it was out of a need to have quick recipes that the *Cooking on the Go* was created.

Since that book was printed, many things in my life have changed and I find myself cooking less and less! Not because I want to cook less, but because I don't have the time to cook the way I use to cook. I do not think I am alone. It was out of this feeling of frustration that this cookbook, my fourth and favorite, was created!

This cookbook is dedicated to those women and men who love home cooked food but don't have the time to prepare it. It is designed to help make grocery shopping easy, cooking fast, and mealtime enjoyable without spending hours in the kitchen.

The recipes in this book have only 4 ingredients in them plus salt, pepper and water! The way I figure it, if you don't have salt, pepper, and water, you have no business in the kitchen anyway! The recipes are cross referenced by ingredients so that you can quickly locate a recipe that goes with the ingredients you have in the refrigerator!

I have been working on this book and creating short cuts to my favorite recipes for the past ten years. My hope is that you will enjoy cooking again and that at your house, fast food will have new meaning!

Happy Cooking,
Nancy Turner Welch

Copyright © 1992

NTW Enterprises
101 Summit Drive
Greer, S.C. 29651

Contents

Appetizers and Soups

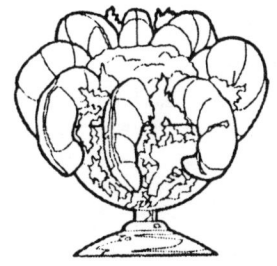

Egg Sandwich

7 eggs, hard boiled
5-3/4 oz. jar olives

1/3 c. chopped nuts
Mayonnaise

Chop eggs, add other ingredients. Add enough mayonnaise to hold together. Spread on bread. May also be used as a spread on crackers.

Appetizer Cheese Biscuits

2 sticks margarine
1/2 lb. grated sharp cheese
(2-1/2 to 3 c.)
2 c. plain flour

1 tsp. salt
1/4 tsp. pepper
2 c. Rice Krispies

Combine butter, cheese, salt and pepper. Add flour a little at a time. Add Rice Krispies last and mix well. Form into small balls. Place on cookie sheet and flatten with floured spoon. Bake at 350° until light brown. Store in covered container. Biscuits will keep for 2 weeks or more.

Chile-Ham Turnovers

1 (4 oz.) can chopped green
chiles, well drained
1 (2-1/8 oz.) can deviled ham
1/2 c. (2 oz.) shredded
Monterey Jack cheese

1 (10 oz.) can refrigerated
flaky biscuits
Water

Combine first 3 ingredients, stirring well; set aside. Cut each biscuit in half; on a lightly floured surface, roll each half to a 3-inch circle. Place 1 teaspoon ham mixture in center of each circle; moisten edges of circles with water. Fold circles in half, and press edges together with a fork. Prick tops with a fork. Place on an ungreased baking sheet; bake at 400° for 12 minutes or until lightly browned. Yield: 20 appetizer servings.

Stuffed Celery

1 (3 oz.) pkg. cream cheese,
    softened
1/2 tsp. Worcestershire sauce

1/2 tsp. lemon juice
1 tbsp. finely chopped nuts

Blend cream cheese, Worcestershire, and lemon juice. Stir in nuts. Spread about 1 tablespoon into hollow of 3 inch long pieces of celery. Serve.

Yogurt Snack

1 (8 oz.) carton plain low-fat
    yogurt
1/3 c. orange juice

2 tsp. honey
1 c. sliced banana, frozen

Combine first 3 ingredients in container of an electric blender; process until smooth. Gradually add banana slices; process until mixture is smooth. Yield: 2-1/4 cups (121 calories per 3/4-cup serving).

Chili Dip

1 (15 oz.) can chili without
    beans
1 (8 oz.) pkg. cream cheese,
    softened

1/2 c. green chile sauce or
    jalapeno salsa
1 (2-1/4 oz.) can sliced black
    olives, drained

Combine chili and cream cheese in a medium saucepan. Cook over low heat until cheese melts, stirring occasionally. Stir in sauce and olives. Serve dip warm with assorted chips. Yield: 3 cups.

Sausage-Cheese Turnovers

10 (1 oz.) link sausages
2 oz. sharp cheddar cheese
2 tbsp. cornmeal

1 (11 oz.) can refrigerated
   biscuits

Cook sausage in a skillet until browned; drain well. Set aside. Cut cheese to 2 x 1/2 x 1/4 inch strips; set aside. Roll each biscuit to a 4 inch circle on wax paper sprinkled with cornmeal. Place a cheese strip and a sausage in center of each biscuit. Fold over, and pinch edges to seal. Press edges together with a fork dipped in flour. Place on a lightly greased baking sheet; bake at 400° for 10 minutes. Yield: 10 servings.

Cream Cheese Dip

1 (3 oz.) pkg. cream cheese,
   softened
1/2 c. commercial sour cream

1/4 c. strawberry preserves
1 tbsp. lemon juice

Beat cream cheese at medium speed of an electric mixer until creamy. Add sour cream, strawberry preserves, and juice, mixing until light and fluffy. Spoon into serving dish. Serve with fresh fruit. Yield: 1-1/3 cups.

Sugar Snap Dip

1/4 lb. fresh Sugar Snap peas,
   divided
1 (3 oz.) pkg. cream cheese,
   softened

1/2 c. commercial clam dip
1/2 tsp. Worcestershire sauce

Trim ends from 1/4 pound peas. Position knife blade in food processor bowl; add 1/2 of prepared peas. Process 5 to 10 seconds. Stop processor, and scrape down sides of bowl with a rubber spatula. Process an additional 10 seconds or until peas are finely chopped. Drain and set aside. Beat cream cheese at high speed of an electric mixer until fluffy; stir in chopped peas, clam dip, and Worcestershire sauce. Serve with additional peas. Yield: 1 cup.

Salami-Cheese Snacks

2 (3 oz.) pkg. cream
    cheese, softened

1 (6 oz.) pkg. 3-in. round
    hard salami

Spread 1 package of cream cheese evenly on 5 slices of salami; stack and top with another slice of salami. Cover and chill 4 hours. Cut into 8 wedges. For log-shaped snacks, spread remaining cream cheese evenly on each remaining slice of salami. Roll each slice jelly roll fashion; secure with wooden picks. Cover and chill. Yield: about 1-1/2 dozen.

Sandwich Spread

1 sm. jar (1/2 pt.) Miracle
    Whip

1 can tuna (6-1/2 oz.)
1/2 lb. Velveeta cheese

In top of double boiler heat salad dressing and cheese until melted. Add flaked tuna fish. Mix well and store in refrigerator. Serves 6.

Cucumber Sandwich Filling

1 (8 oz.) pkg. cream cheese,
    softened
1 tbsp. Italian salad dressing mix

2 tbsp. milk
1 lge. cucumber, sliced

Combine first 3 ingredients, mixing well. Spread mixture on bread, and top with cucumber slices. Yield: 6 servings.

Sausage Appetizers

1 pkg. Bisquick mix

1/2 lb. sausage, uncooked

Mix Bisquick according to directions on package. Roll out as if making biscuits. Break uncooked sausage apart and crumble on top of dough. Roll up, jelly roll style, and slice about 3/4-inch thick. Put on cookie sheet and bake at 375° for 20 to 25 minutes or until dough is brown.

Sweet and Sour Wieners

1 pkg. wieners, cut in small
   pieces
1 jar currant jelly

1 sm. jar prepared mustard
Worcestershire sauce, dash

Melt mustard and jelly over low heat. Add wieners; bring to a boil. Simmer 1 hour. Serve hot with picks in chafing dish.

Spinach Dip

1 (10 oz.) pkg. frozen chopped
   spinach, thawed, well
   drained, do not cook
1 c. sour cream

1 tbsp. mayonnaise
1 (4 oz.) sm. pkg. Ranch
   Style buttermilk dressing
   mix

Mix above. Chill and serve with corn chips.

Quick Appetizers

8 oz. pkg. cream cheese
Crackers

Green pepper jelly or
Pickapeppa sauce

Place chilled cream cheese on a serving plate. Spread green pepper jelly or a generous amount of Pickapeppa sauce over the cream cheese. Serve with crackers. (Pickapeppa is usually found in the gourmet section of the grocery store.)

Hot Artichoke Dip

1 (14 oz.) can artichoke
   hearts, finely chopped
1 c. Hellmann's mayonnaise

6 to 8 oz. Parmesan cheese,
   grated
Cayenne, Tabasco, salt to taste

Mix all thoroughly. Bake at 350° for 30 minutes. Serve warm in ovenproof dish with plain crackers. Serves 20 to 25.

Buttery Toasted Pecans

1/2 c. butter
1/2 tsp. salt

4 c. pecan halves

Place butter in a 15 x 10 x 2-inch jelly roll pan. Heat at 325° for 5 minutes or until butter melts. Add pecans; stir until well coated. Sprinkle with salt; return to oven. Bake at 325° for 40 minutes or until toasted, stirring every 10 minutes. Drain on paper towels. Yield: 4 cups.

Glazed Nuts

3-3/4 c. pecan pieces
1/2 c. sugar
1/4 c. vegetable oil

3 c. slivered almonds
1/8 tsp. seasoned salt or
   reg. salt

Combine all ingredients in a large heavy skillet; cook over medium heat about 5 minutes or until golden brown, stirring constantly. Immediately spread nuts in a thin layer on a jelly roll pan; cool. Stir occasionally to separate nuts. Yield: 6-3/4 cups.

Cheese Wafers

2 sticks margarine
2 c. sharp grated cheese
2 c. flour

1 tsp. salt
1/4 tsp. cayenne pepper
2 c. Rice Krispies

Cream first two ingredients. Add flour, salt, cayenne. Add to creamed mixture. Fold in Rice Krispies. Chill, drop by teaspoons on cookie sheet. Bake at 350° for 12 to 15 minutes.

Olive Balls

1 glass jar of sharp cheese
3 tbsp. soft butter or margarine

3/4 c. self-rising flour
1 jar stuffed olives

Mix ingredients and form into balls around a stuffed olive. Bake at 350° for 15 minutes. Serve hot if possible.

Cheese Ball or Log

1/2 lb. cheddar cheese (grated)
16 oz. cream cheese (softened)
2 tbsp. grated onion
1 tsp. salt
Finely chopped pecans

Mix all ingredients well and roll into a ball or log. Roll in finely chopped pecans. Wrap. Will keep several days.

Hot Pecan Crackers

Sharp cheddar cheese (grated)
Ritz crackers
Dash of Tabasco
Pecan halves

Mix Tabasco with grated cheese. Spread on Ritz crackers. Top with pecan halves. Pop under broiler just until bubbly.

Hot Velveeta Cheese Dip

1 lb. Velveeta cheese, melted
1 can chili tomatoes (10 oz.)

Melt cheese on top of stove. Stir in can of chili tomatoes. Heat until just before boiling. Transfer to chafing dish and keep hot. Use corn chips, vegetables, potato chips or crackers to dip.

Bacon Roll-Ups

1 (8 oz.) pkg. soft cream cheese
with chives and onion
25 slices bacon, halved
crosswise
1 tbsp. milk or mayonnaise
25 slices mixed grain sandwich
bread, crusts removed;
halved

Combine cream cheese and milk, stirring until of spreading consistency. Spread 1 scant teaspoon cream cheese mixture on each slice of bread; roll tightly. Wrap each roll-up with bacon; secure with wooden pick. Place on broiler pan. Bake at 350° for 30 minutes, turning if necessary to prevent overbrowning. Garnish with parsley, if desired. (Roll-ups may be assembled ahead and frozen. To serve, thaw overnight in refrigerator; bake at 350° for 30-40 minutes.) Yield: 4 dozen.

Pineapple Roll-Ups

1 fresh pineapple or 1 (20 oz.)
   can pineapple chunks,
   drained

1 lb. bacon, partially cooked

Cut each bacon slice in half. Cut pineapple into bite-sized chunks. Wrap each pineapple chunk with half slice of bacon; secure with wooden pick. Place on broiler rack. Broil until bacon is crisp, turning once. (To grill: Thread wrapped pineapple chunks onto small skewers. Grill 3-4 inches from hot coals for 3-5 minutes, until bacon is crisp; turn once or twice.) Serves 16-20.

Water Chestnuts Wrapped in Bacon

1 (5 oz.) can water chestnuts,
   drained and halved
4 slices bacon, cut in half
   crosswise and lengthwise

1/4 c. soy sauce
1/4 c. sugar

Marinate water chestnuts 30 minutes in soy sauce. Roll each chestnut half in sugar. Wrap with bacon; secure with cocktail pick. Arrange on broiler pan. Bake at 400° for 30 minutes. Drain on absorbent toweling. (May be made ahead and reheated at 350° for 5 minutes.)

Cheese Straws

1 lb. New York sharp cheddar
   cheese, grated
1 tsp. salt

1 c. butter or margarine
3 c. sifted flour
1/2 tsp. red pepper

Cream cheese and margarine. Add dry ingredients; mix well. Pack into cookie press. Press onto ungreased baking sheet. Bake at 350° for 10-12 minutes. Transfer to wire racks to cool or serve warm. Yield: 3 dozen.

Cucumber Dip

1 lg. (8 oz.) pkg. cream
    cheese, soft
1 lg. cucumber

Dash of Worcestershire sauce
Dash of garlic salt

Peel cucumber and grate. Mix with other ingredients. Blend with mixer. Serve with crackers.

Fried Cheese

Cheddar cheese, cut into
    3/4-in. cubes
2 eggs, beaten

3/4 c. dry bread crumbs
Hot oil

Dip cheese in egg. Coat with crumbs. Repeat until all cubes are coated. Put in refrigerator for at least 20 minutes. Fry in deep oil for 1 to 2 minutes, until lightly browned.

Ham and Cheese Delights

1 can crescent rolls
Ham slices

Cheese
Mustard with celery seed

Separate crescent rolls. Place mustard, ham and cheese on each roll. Roll crescents as directed on package, being sure all cheese is covered. Bake as directed. Serve whole or cut vertically before baking and serve as appetizers.

Egg Dip

1 c. dairy sour cream
1 slice bacon, cooked crisp,
    drained and crumbled,
    optional

1 pkg. (0.56 oz.) onion-bacon
    dip mix
3 hard-cooked eggs, chopped

Mix sour cream and dip mix together until well blended. Fold in chopped eggs. Cover and chill to blend flavors. Garnish with crumbled bacon, if desired. Serve with raw vegetable dippers or crackers and chips. Makes about 1-1/2 cups.

Ham Roll-Ups

Cream cheese, softened
Mayonnaise, small amount

Olives, chopped
Thin ham slices

Cream mayonnaise and cream cheese in blender. Add chopped olives. Spread on ham slices and roll up. Secure with toothpick.

Mustard Dip for Vegetables

1-1/2 c. mayonnaise
2 tbsp. lemon juice

1/4 c. sugar
2-1/2 tbsp. mustard

Mix sugar and lemon juice until partially dissolved. Add all other ingredients, and mix well. If you want it sweeter, use sugar to taste. Excellent dip for fried cheese and vegetables.

Sausage-Bacon Roll-Ups

12 slices bacon, halved
  crosswise
12 slices white bread

1/2 lb. bulk pork sausage
1 (8 oz.) pkg. cream cheese,
  softened

Cook bacon until transparent; drain well on paper towels, and set aside. Cook sausage over medium heat until browned, stirring to crumble; drain. Combine sausage and cream cheese; stir well, and set aside. Trim crust from bread; cut slices in half. Spread cream cheese mixture over bread. Starting with short end, roll up each slice of bread, jelly roll fashion. Wrap each with bacon, and secure with a wooden pick. Place roll-ups on an ungreased baking sheet. Bake at 350° for 15 minutes. Yield: 2 dozen. **Note:** Roll-ups may be frozen before adding bacon. Remove from freezer (do not thaw); wrap with bacon, and secure with wooden picks. Bake as directed.

Crab Sandwiches

1 (10 oz.) pkg. refrigerated
   biscuits
1 (8 oz.) pkg. frozen crab meat

1/2 c. grated sharp cheddar
   cheese
3 tbsp. mayonnaise

Separate biscuits. Pat each into a 3-1/2 inch round. Arrange half on greased baking sheet. Mix crab, drained, with cheese and mayonnaise. Spread on biscuits. Top with the rest of the biscuits. Brush tops with melted butter. Let stand 15-20 minutes. Bake at 425° for 15-20 minutes, or until browned. Makes 5 sandwiches.

Spinach Vegetable Dip

1 pkg. frozen chopped (10 oz.)
   spinach, thawed and drained
1 c. mayonnaise

1/2 c. chopped onion
1/2 tsp. salt
2 tsp. parsley

Put all ingredients in blender. Blend on high for about 2 minutes. Serve with raw vegetables. Make the day before to enhance the flavor.

Mexican Dip

1 lg. can tomatoes and
   green chilies
1 pkg. spiced dried beef

1 (10 oz.) pkg. sharp cheddar
   cheese
1 (8 oz.) pkg. Velveeta cheese

Melt together cheeses on low heat, stirring every 15 minutes. When melted, add tomatoes and chilies; stir. Chop beef and add to mixture. Serve in chafing dish with taco chips or Doritos.

Crab-Cheese Rolls

4 tbsp. butter, divided
1/2 lb. Velveeta cheese
1 lb. crabmeat, cut in pieces

2 loaves Pepperidge Farm
thin-sliced white bread

Melt in double boiler butter, cheese and crabmeat. Remove crusts of bread. Roll very thin with a rolling pin. Spread with mixture. Roll up and freeze. When ready to serve, cut each roll in half and spread with melted butter. Defrost and bake at 300° for 10 to 15 minutes. Makes 60 to 80 rolls.

Shrimp Paste

5 lb. raw shrimp
2 tsp. salt in water
1 lg. Bermuda onion, peeled
and quartered

1 pt. Miracle Whip salad
dressing
Juice of 1 lemon
Salt and pepper to taste

Boil shrimp for 5 minutes in a covered pot, using just enough salted water to cover. Large shrimp may require an extra few minutes cooking time. Drain shrimp and peel. Put shrimp and onion through meat grinder or in food processor and process until coarse. Mix well with salad dressing, lemon juice, salt and pepper. May be used on crackers or made into sandwiches.

Cheese Hot Bits

1 c. flour
2 c. New York cheese, grated
1/2 c. butter

1/4 tsp. salt
1/2 tsp. cayenne pepper
1 c. pecans, chopped

Cream flour, cheese, butter, salt and cayenne pepper with hand. Add nuts and cream until they are well mixed. Roll in logs. Wrap in wax paper. Chill overnight. Slice thin and bake on ungreased pan for 10 to 15 minutes in 325° oven. Do not brown. Sprinkle salt on wafers when they are first taken from the oven. May be frozen.

Bacon and Cheese Canapes

1 lb. lean bacon
1 party loaf rye or
    pumpernickel
1 c. mayonnaise
8 oz. sharp cheddar cheese

Fry bacon very crisp and break into small pieces. Shred cheese and combine with bacon. Add mayonnaise. Put in refrigerator until an hour before the party. Spread mixture on bread slices and return to refrigerator. When ready to serve, put into 350° oven for about 10 minutes or until cheese melts.

Swiss Sandwich Puffs

1/2 c. mayonnaise
1/4 c. chopped onion
1 loaf tiny rye slices, 32 slices
8 slices Swiss cheese

Combine mayonnaise and onion. Spread on rye slices. Top each with 1/4 slice cheese. Broil 2 to 3 minutes.

Cream Cheese Spread

8 oz. cream cheese
1 c. sweetened mashed
    strawberries
1/4 c. powdered sugar

Combine all ingredients until creamy. Use to spread on slices of Strawberry Bread. May be served with other breads or un-iced cakes.

Creamy Blue Cheese Spread

1 (3 oz.) pkg. cream cheese,
    softened
1/4 c. butter or margarine,
    softened
1 (3 oz.) pkg. blue cheese,
    softened
1 tbsp. brandy

Combine cream cheese, blue cheese, and butter; beat at medium speed of an electric mixer until smooth. Add brandy, mixing well. Serve with crackers or sliced apples or pears. Yield: 1 cup.

Cream of Curry Soup

1 qt. chicken broth
2 tbsp. curry powder
4 egg yolks

1 c. heavy cream
Salt and pepper

Bring chicken broth and curry powder to a slow boil and cook 10 minutes. Mix the egg yolks with cream, salt and pepper and add to the boiling chicken broth, stirring all together until the boiling point is reached. Cool. Set in refrigerator. Serve thoroughly chilled in cups. Serves 8.

Clam Chowder

2 c. clams
2 c. onion
2 c. white potatoes

4 qts. water
6 tsp. salt
7-1/2 tbsp. Lea & Perrins sauce

Put water on to boil. Grind clams, onion and potatoes. Add to boiling water. Let boil for 15 minutes. Add other ingredients and simmer for about 2 to 3 hours. Makes one gallon.

New England Clam Chowder

1 can cream of celery soup
2 cans cream of potato soup

2 soup cans milk
2 cans minced or chopped clams

Mix all the ingredients together, heat until piping hot and serve. Makes 4 to 6 servings.

Cold Lemon Soup

1 tbsp. lemon juice
1 egg yolk

4 tbsp. Parmesan cheese
4 c. chicken consomme

Combine lemon juice, egg yolk and cheese. Heat consomme. When it reaches a boil, whisk lemon mixture into it. Chill. Top with slice of lemon. Serves 4.

Curried Tomato Soup

1/4 c. sliced green onions
2 tbsp. melted butter
2 (10-3/4 oz.) cans tomato
   soup, undiluted

2-1/2 c. water
3/4 tsp. curry powder

Saute onion in butter until lightly browned. Add tomato soup, water and curry powder. (Add more powder to suit taste). Heat thoroughly, stirring constantly. Serves 4-6. Serve cold or hot.

Cream Cheese Soup

4 (3 oz.) pkg. cream cheese
2 c. beef consomme

3/4 tsp. curry powder
Red caviar or tiny shrimp

Blend the cream cheese, consomme and curry powder in blender until smooth. Correct seasonings. Chill. Place a teaspoon of red caviar or 6 shrimp in each cup as served. Serves 6. (This is a delicious cold soup. May be jellied as a salad by adding 1 envelope of gelatin to each pint of liquid.)

Cold Fresh Tomato Soup

12 lg. tomatoes, ripe
2 sm. onions, grated
2 tsp. salt

1 tbsp. sugar
1 tsp. dried basil
1 tsp. black pepper

Drop tomatoes into boiling water for 1 minute. Remove and peel. Mash or grind tomatoes through a medium grinder. Add onions. Stir in salt, black pepper, sugar and dried basil. Chill thoroughly. Taste for seasoning. Add more of the seasoning if necessary. Garnish with a spoonful of sour cream. Serves 8 to 12.

Cold Squash Soup

1 med. onion, chopped
1 lb. yellow crookneck squash, sliced

1-1/2 c. chicken stock
1/2 c. sour cream
Salt and pepper to taste

Cook onion and squash in 1 cup of chicken stock about 15 minutes or until soft. Puree in blender. Transfer to bowl. Stir in 1/2 cup of the chicken stock and sour cream. Season to taste. Chill thoroughly and serve garnished with chopped fresh dill. Serves 4.

Gazpacho

1 bowl of leftover tossed salad with any kind of dressing already on it

1 can tomatoes
Sour cream
Salt & pepper to taste

Put tossed salad into blender or food processor and blend until nearly liquid. Add can of tomatoes and blend a few seconds more. Chill in refrigerator. When ready to serve, pour into cups or bowls and top with a spoonful of sour cream.

Beverages

Egg Nog

12 lg. eggs, separated
1 pt. whipping cream, whipped
3/4 c. bourbon
1-3/4 c. sugar

Whip cream and set aside. Wash beaters. Beat egg whites till stiff but not dry, adding sugar gradually. In large bowl beat egg yolks until light colored, adding whiskey gradually. Fold cream into yolk mixture using a spatula, then fold in whites. Serves 8.

Sparkling Apple Cider

1 (12 oz.) can frozen apple juice concentrate, thawed and undiluted
1 (23 oz.) bottle sparkling mineral water, chilled

Combine apple juice concentrate and mineral water, stirring gently. Serve immediately over crushed ice. Yield: about 4-1/2 cups.

Lime Punch

2 pkg. lemon-lime regular Kool-Aid
2 c. sugar
2 qt. water
1 (46 oz.) pineapple juice
1 qt. ginger ale

Dissolve sugar and Kool-Aid in lukewarm water. Add rest of water then pineapple juice, and chill. Put chilled ginger ale in when ready to serve. Serves 36.

Apple Punch

3 bottles apple juice (1 qt. each)
3 tsp. whole cloves (put in bag)
1/2 c. candy cinnamon hearts

Pour apple juice in a pot. Add cinnamon hearts and cloves. Heat until candy is melted. When punch is hot take out bag of cloves. This recipe is good hot or cold. Keeps several days. Serves 20 to 25 people.

Apple Punch

1 gal. apple juice
1/2 gal. orange juice

2 liter bottle ginger ale
Food coloring (red or green)

Combine all ingredients and serve in a punch bowl over crushed ice.

Orange Blush

2 (6 oz.) cans frozen orange
   juice, thawed and
   undiluted

2 c. cranberry juice
1/2 c. sugar
4 c. ginger ale

Combine orange juice, cranberry juice and sugar. Stir until sugar dissolves. Chill. Just before serving, add ginger ale. Serve over crushed ice.

Apricot Iced Tea

4 c. boiling water
6 tea bags
3/4 to 1 c. sugar

1 can (12 oz.) apricot nectar
Juice of 3 to 4 lemons

Make tea, leaving bags in for 4-5 minutes. Add other ingredients and chill.

Microwave Iced Tea

2 c. water
2 family sized tea bags

1-1/2 c. sugar

Place tea bags in water, and microwave on high for 5 minutes. Add to gallon container while hot and dissolve the sugar. Finish filling container with cold water.

Brandy Alexander

3 oz. brandy
3 oz. Creme de Cacao

Blender of vanilla ice cream
(about 1/2 gallon)

Mix above in blender. Serves 6. Nice in summer in place of dessert.

Vineyard Punch

1 (6 oz.) can frozen orange juice
1 (6 oz.) can frozen lemonade
1 (28 oz.) bottle ginger ale

1 (6 oz.) can limeade
4 c. very cold water

Mix orange juice, lemonade, limeade and water. Put in punch bowl with ice. Add ginger ale. Yields: 14 6-ounce servings.

Russian Instant Tea

2-1/4 c. Tang
1/2 c. instant tea,
    pre-sweetened

1 tsp. cinnamon
1/2 tsp. cloves

Mix and store in jar with lid. To serve: 2 teaspoons to 1 cup hot water.

Banana Drink

2 med. bananas
1 sm. can frozen orange juice
ice cubes

1 sm. can crushed pineapple
    with liquid

Combine bananas, orange juice, and pineapple in blender. Fill with ice cubes and blend until ice is almost dissolved. Serve in chilled glasses. NOTE: 1 sm. orange juice can of Peach Schnapps can be added.

Instant Cocoa

4 c. nonfat dry milk
1 c. cocoa

2 c. sugar
1/2 tsp. salt

Mix and sift together. Store in tightly covered jar. To make beverage, use 1/4 cup mix to 1 cup boiling water. Stir until smooth.

Chocolate Mint Patty Punch

1/4 c. white creme de menthe
1/4 c. creme de cacao

1 qt. chocolate ice cream

Put liquers in blender. Add ice cream a spoonful at a time, blending smoothly after each addition. Pour into stemmed glasses and serve immediately. Garnish with mint sprigs, chocolate curls and/or crushed peppermint candy. Serves 6.

Sparkling Cranberry Juice

1 (12 oz.) can frozen cranberry
   juice concentrate, thawed
   and undiluted

1 (23 oz.) bottle sparkling
   mineral water, chilled

Combine cranberry juice concentrate and mineral water, stirring gently. Serve immediately over crushed ice. Yield: 4-1/2 cups.

Instant Russian Tea

1/2 c. instant tea
1-1/4 c. sugar
2 c. Tang

1/2 tsp. cloves
1 tsp. cinnamon
2 instant lemonade envelopes

Combine all ingredients. Store in tightly covered container. Put 3 heaping teaspoons to mug. Add hot water. Stir.

Cafe Vienna

1/2 c. instant coffee
2/3 c. sugar

2/3 c. nonfat dry milk powder
1/2 tsp. cinnamon

Combine all ingredients. Place 4 rounded teaspoons in cup and add 3/4 to 1 cup boiling water. Yield: about 2 cups of dry mix, or enough to make 20 cups of coffee.

Instant Russian Tea

1 (18 oz.) jar Tang
1-1/2 c. sugar
1/2 c. instant tea

1 tsp. ground cloves
1 tsp. ground cinnamon

Mix all ingredients well and store in an airtight jar. Use 1-1/2 teaspoons tea mix to 1 cup boiling water.

Instant Hot Chocolate Mix

1 (44.8 oz.) box nonfat dry
   milk
1 (16 oz.) jar coffee creamer

1 (2 lb.) box Nestle Quik
1 (1 lb.) box powdered sugar

Mix together in large container. Then store dry in jars. Makes about 2-1/2 gallons dry mixture, enough for around 100 cups. To make each cup of hot chocolate, use 1/3 cup instant mix to a cup of boiling water.

Cafe Cappuccino

1/2 c. instant coffee
3/4 c. sugar
1 c. nonfat dry milk powder

1/2 tsp. dried orange peel,
   crushed

Combine all ingredients. Place 4 rounded teaspoons in cup and add 3/4 to 1 cup boiling water. Yield: about 2 cups of dry mix, or enough to make 20 cups of coffee.

Swiss Mocha

1/2 c. instant coffee
1/2 c. sugar

1 c. nonfat dry milk powder
2 tbsp. unsweetened cocoa

Combine all ingredients. Place 4 rounded teaspoons in cup and add 3/4 to 1 cup of boiling water. Yield: about 2 cups dry mix, or enough to make 20 cups of coffee.

Cheerwine Punch

2 lit. Cheerwine
2 lit. ginger ale

1 (46 oz.) pineapple juice

Mix ingredients. Add ice & serve.

Pineapple Punch

1 (46 oz.) can Pineapple juice
1 tsp. almond flavoring

1 lg. can frozen lemonade
1 qt. ginger ale

Pour first 3 ingredients into gallon jug. Fill with water. When ready to serve, put 1 gallon of punch to 1 qt. ginger ale.

Mock Champagne

Equal amounts of white grape juice & ginger ale. Chill before serving.

Breads

Egg Popovers

2 eggs
1 c. flour

1 c. milk
1/2 tsp. salt

Combine eggs, flour, milk and salt. Beat mixture thoroughly with rotary beater. Pour batter into 6 well-greased muffin cups 3/4 full. Place in **cold** oven. Set temperature at 400° and bake 30 minutes. **Do not** open while baking.

7-Up Biscuits

2 c. sifted flour
1 tsp. salt
3/4 c. cold 7-Up beverage

4 tsp. baking powder
1/2 c. solid shortening

Sift flour, baking powder, and salt into bowl. Cut in shortening, blending until mixture is like coarse cornmeal. Add **cold** 7-Up all at once. Stir with fork only until ingredients are evenly moistened. Turn onto lightly floured surface. Knead quickly 8-10 times. Roll to 3/4-inch thickness. Allow dough to rest 5 minutes. Cut with floured biscuit cutter. Place on ungreased baking sheet; brush with melted butter if desired. Bake at 450° for 10 minutes or until golden brown. Serve immediately. Makes 12 biscuits.

Baking Powder Biscuits

2 c. sifted all-purpose flour
3 tsp. baking powder
1/2 tsp. salt

1/3 c. shortening
3/4 to 1 c. milk

Sift flour, baking powder, and salt together into a large mixing bowl. Cut in shortening with a pastry blender or two forks. Add enough milk to make a soft dough. Mix with fork just until all dry ingredients are moistened. Pat out to 1/2-inch thickness on lightly floured board or pastry cloth; cut with a round 2-inch cutter. Place 1/2-inch apart on ungreased baking sheet; brush tops with melted butter or margarine. Bake at 450° about 15 minutes. Yield: 12 to 14 2-inch biscuits.

Sweet Potato Biscuits

1 (16 oz.) can drained sweet
    potatoes
1/4 c. milk

1 tbsp. sugar
1-1/2 c. biscuit mix

Combine potatoes, milk and sugar and beat until smooth. Add biscuit mix; stir with a fork until moistened. Turn out and knead 5 times. Roll out 1/2 inch thick and cut with 2-1/2 inch cutter. Bake on ungreased baking sheet at 450° for approximately 12 minutes. Makes 10-12 biscuits.

Cheese Biscuits

1/2 lb. margarine, softened
1/2 lb. New York extra sharp
    cheddar cheese, grated
2 c. all-purpose flour

Dash of red pepper or black
    pepper
Pecan halves

Mix all ingredients thoroughly. Divide — make into two long rolls about 1-1/2-inch diameter. Wrap in wax paper. Chill overnight, or longer. Slice about 1/4-inch thick. Place on greased baking sheet. Put pecan half on top. Bake at 350° for 10 to 15 minutes. Don't let them get too brown because they darken more when cooling. They keep well if covered. You can freeze this dough. It will keep several weeks.

Rolls

1-1/2 c. self-rising flour
3/4 c. sweet milk

3 tbsp. mayonnaise
1 tsp. sugar

Mix all ingredients quickly. Fill greased muffin cups half full. Do **not** let rise. Bake 375° until brown. Makes 12.

Beer Bread

3 c. self-rising flour
2 tbsp. sugar

1 (12 oz.) can beer (room temp.)

Mix all ingredients. Put into a greased 9 x 5'' loaf pan and let rise 30 minutes. Bake 1 hour at 450°. Take out of pan and butter all over while still hot. Wrap in a clean cloth.

French Bread

1 pkg. rapid rise yeast
4 c. bread flour
1 tsp. salt
2 tbsp. butter or margarine, melted

1 c. warm water (105° to 115°)
1 tbsp. sugar
2/3 to 1 c. warm water (105° to 115°)

Dissolve yeast in 1 cup warm water in a small bowl; let stand 5 minutes. Combine flour, sugar, and salt in a large mixing bowl. Stir in yeast and enough remaining water to make a soft dough. Cover and let rise in a warm place (85°), free from drafts, 30 minutes or until doubled in bulk. Turn dough out onto a heavily floured surface; knead until smooth and elastic (about 5 minutes). Divide dough in half. Shape each half into an oval on a heavily floured surface. Fold over lengthwise, and flatten with open hand. Fold it again, and roll with palms of hands to a 15 x 2-inch loaf. Twist and place loaves in greased French bread pans. Brush with butter. Cover and let rise in a warm place (85°), free from drafts, about 30 minutes or until doubled in bulk. Bake at 400° for 40 minutes or until loaves sound hollow when tapped. Yield: 2 loaves.

Garlic Bread: Slice French bread into 1-inch slices. Combine 6 tablespoons softened butter, 1/4 to 1/2 teaspoon garlic salt and 1-1/2 tablespoons grated Parmesan cheese; spread butter mixture between bread slices. Wrap loaf in aluminum foil, and bake at 350° for 10 minutes or until thoroughly heated. Yield: enough spread for 2 loaves.

Spoon Bread

2 c. milk, boiling
1/2 c. white cornmeal
2 tbsp. butter

1/4 tsp. salt
4 egg yolks, beaten
4 egg whites, beaten

Slowly stir cornmeal into milk. Let simmer 5 minutes and stir well to prevent lumps. Add butter and salt. Remove from heat and cool. Stir in egg yolks; fold in egg whites. Turn into deep well-greased 1-quart casserole that has been heated. Bake 25 minutes at 350°.

Cornmeal Muffins

2 c. cornmeal
1 tsp. salt
1-1/2 c. buttermilk

1 tsp. baking soda
1 egg, beaten

Combine cornmeal, baking soda and salt in a medium bowl, mixing well. Combine egg and buttermilk, mixing well. Add to dry ingredients, stirring until batter is smooth. Place a well-greased cast-iron muffin pan in a 500° oven for 2 minutes or until very hot. Remove pan from oven; spoon batter into pan, filling three-fourths full. Bake at 500° for 9 to 10 minutes or until lightly browned. Yield: 16 muffins. NOTE: If using regular muffin pan, bake at 450° for 10 to 12 minutes.

Butter Biscuits Sticks

1/2 c. margarine or butter
1-1/4 c. milk

3 c. self-rising flour

Melt margarine in 2-quart oblong baking dish. Combine flour and milk to form soft dough. Turn on floured board; knead several times. Roll into 14 x 7-inch rectangle. Cut in half lengthwise, then crosswise into 1/2-inch-wide strips. Turn each strip in melted margarine; place close together in baking dish. Bake at 425° for 10 minutes or until brown. Yield: 14-18 biscuits sticks.

Blue Cheese Biscuits

1/4 c. butter or margarine
1 (10 oz.) pkg. refrigerated
  biscuits

2 tbsp. crumbled blue cheese
1 tsp. lemon juice

Combine butter and blue cheese in a small saucepan; cook over low heat, stirring constantly, until butter and cheese melt. Stir in lemon juice, and cook over medium heat 1 minute or until slightly thickened. Pour mixture into a 9-inch round cakepan. Cut each biscuit into quarters, and place on top of mixture. Bake at 400° for 10 to 12 minutes or until browned. Yield: 10 servings.

Buttermilk Biscuits

2 c. self-rising flour
1/4 tsp. baking soda

4 tbsp. shortening
3/4 to 1 c. buttermilk

Mix flour and soda. Cut shortening into flour until mixture resembles cornmeal. Add buttermilk; mix to form soft dough. (May be done to this point in food processor, using steel blade.) Turn onto floured board; knead lightly several times until dough is smooth. Roll to desired thickness. Cut with floured biscuit cutter. Place on lightly greased baking sheet. Bake at 450° for 15 minutes or until golden brown. Yield: 12 biscuits.

Cheesy Sausage Biscuits

2 pkg. Bisquick baking mix
2/3 c. milk

1 lb. sausage
1 c. grated cheddar cheese

Preheat oven to 375°. Prepare mix by adding milk, mix well. Add cheese and sausage to biscuit mixture. Beat by hand until well combined. Shape into balls and bake for 15-20 minutes. Makes 2 dozen.

Quick Donuts

Canned biscuits   Oil
Powdered sugar   Cinnamon sugar

Buy the least expensive canned biscuits, not the buttered ones or the flaked ones. Cut a hole in center of each biscuit with the screw-on top of the 2 liter soft drink bottle. Heat oil in deep fryer or about 1'' deep in frying pan. Drop donuts and holes into hot oil. Turn once; drain on paper towels and sprinkle with powdered sugar or cinnamon and sugar.

Breakfast Buns

1 (10 oz.) can Hungry Jack biscuits
1/2 c. cinnamon sugar
1/4 c. margarine, melted
10 tsp. strawberry or other preserves

Separate dough into 10 biscuits. Dip both sides of biscuits in melted margarine, then in cinnamon sugar mixture. Place on ungreased cookie sheet. With thumb, make deep indentation in center of each biscuit and fill with one teaspoon preserves. Bake at 375° for 15 to 20 minutes or until golden brown. Serve warm.

Shortbread

3 c. plain flour   2 sticks butter
1/2 c. + 2 tbsp. sugar

Mix butter and 1/2 cup sugar; add flour and mix thoroughly. Press into average size cookie tin. Score with knife and sprinkle with 2 tablespoons sugar before baking. Bake at 275° for 1 hour.

Mayonnaise Rolls

1-1/2 c. self-rising flour   3/4 c. milk
3 tbsp. mayonnaise   1 tsp. sugar

Mix ingredients together. Fill greased muffin cups half full. Do NOT let rise. Bake at 375° until brown. Makes 12.

Sour Cream Drop Biscuits

2 c. self-rising flour
Milk to make spooning consistency (about 1/2 to 3/4 cup)
2/3 c. sour cream
4 tbsp. shortening

Mix all ingredients well; drop onto greased pan using teaspoon or tablespoon according to size desired. Bake at 450° for 8-10 minutes. Serve immediately. These are also good toasted the next day for breakfast. If you thought you couldn't make biscuits, try these.

Biscuits

1 c. all-purpose flour
1/2 c. butter
1 (8 oz.) pkg. cream cheese
1/2 tsp. salt

Combine ingredients and pat together. Cut out biscuits and bake at 425° for 15 minutes.

Doris' Biscuits

2 c. self-rising flour
1/2 c. shortening
3/4 c. milk
Flour

Lightly spoon flour into measuring cup. Place flour in a large bowl and cut in shortening with a fork. Stir until moist. Add milk at once. Stir with a fork until mixture leaves the side of the bowl and forms a soft, moist dough. Turn onto floured surface and sprinkle lightly with flour. Knead gently until dough is no longer sticky. Roll dough out to 1/2-inch thickness. Cut with a 2-inch floured biscuit cutter. Bake at 450° on ungreased cookie sheet for 12 minutes or until golden brown.

Bread Sticks

Hot dog buns
Melted butter
Rosemary or thyme

Split hot dog buns lengthwise so that each bun is 4 sticks. Dip into melted butter and sprinkle with either rosemary spice or thyme spice. Lay onto cookie sheet and bake at 300° for 30 to 45 minutes or until toasted. Let cool. Excellent with soups, salads or as an appetizer with beverages.

Banana Loaf Bread

1 pkg. yellow cake mix
4 very ripe bananas, enough
   to make about 1 c. when
   mashed or beaten
2 eggs
1 c. chopped nuts

Beat the eggs well and add the banana pulp to the eggs. You may cut the bananas and beat with electric mixer or blend in a blender with eggs. Add the egg and banana mixture to the yellow cake mix. Add nuts. Put the batter into a greased and floured loaf pan and bake in a slow oven, 350° about one hour. If this batter seems too much for your loaf pan, you might bake the remainder in your cupcake pans.

Monkey Bread

3 cans buttermilk biscuits (10
   per can)
1 stick butter or margarine
1 c. brown sugar
1 c. cinnamon sugar

Cut each biscuit in fourths with scissors. Shake biscuits in a bag with granulated sugar and cinnamon. Layer biscuits into greased tube pan (not one with removable bottom), sprinkle chopped nuts between layers, if desired. (I also enjoy raisins, too). Melt the brown sugar and butter and boil for 1 minute. Pour over biscuits. Bake in a 350° oven for 35 minutes. Let stand for 10 minutes before removing from pan. To serve, just pinch off a piece and eat with fingers. Monkey SEE — Monkey DO! This is delicious and beautiful to serve.

Lipton Onion Soup Sticks

1/2 pkg. onion soup (Lipton's)   1/2 stick butter
White bread

Mix soup and butter and spread on strips of white bread, which
has been cut into finger size bites. Brown under broiler and serve
hot. Serves 8 with other party foods.

Beer Muffins

3 c. Bisquick   12 oz. can beer
1/2 c. sugar

Mix and bake in hot greased muffin tins, 2/3 full, at 400° until done.
Makes about 2 dozen.

Muffin Biscuits

2 c. self-rising flour   4 tbsp. mayonnaise
1 c. milk

Mix together in bowl and fill greased muffin tins 1/2 full. Bake at
450° for 10 minutes. Makes 12.

Sour Cream Muffins

1 c. butter or margarine,   1 (8 oz.) carton commercial
  softened   sour cream
2 c. self-rising flour

Combine butter and sour cream, mixing until smooth. Gradually
stir in flour; stir until blended. Spoon batter into ungreased min-
iature (1-3/4-inch) muffin pans, filling each with 1 tablespoon batter. Bake at 350° for 25 to 30 minutes. Yield: 3 dozen.

Bisquick Muffins

2 c. Bisquick
4 oz. butter or margarine
8 oz. sour cream

1/8 tsp. salt
1 tsp. sugar

Preheat oven to 350°. Spray 36 muffin tins with Pam (small muffin pans). Mix ingredients together and fill cups 3/4 full. Bake 25-30 minutes.

Frozen Strawberry Preserves

4 c. tomatoes, cooked, cut up
   and peeled
4 c. sugar

2 tbsp. lemon juice
2 boxes wild strawberry Jell-O

Mix tomatoes, sugar and lemon juice. Cool 15 minutes and add 2 boxes Jell-O a little at a time. Put in small containers and freeze.

Salads, Dressings, & Sauces

Cooked Apples

3 lb. cooking apples, cored
and quartered
6 tbsp. butter

2 tsp. cinnamon
1 c. sugar
1/2 c. water

Layer apples in a 2-quart casserole. Cover each layer with butter, cinnamon and sugar. Pour water over top. Bake at 350° for 1 hour or until done. Serves 6 to 8.

Baked Fruit Casserole

2 (#2-1/2) cans peaches, drained
1 (#2-1/2) can sliced or chunk
pineapple, drained

3/4 c. brown sugar
1/3 c. margarine or butter

Cut fruit into bite sized pieces. Place in buttered 3 quart casserole. Combine brown sugar & margarine, stir over low heat until margarine has melted. Pour over fruit and bake at 350° about 30 minutes or until mixture is hot and syrup bubbles. Serves 8.

Roquefort Dressing

1 c. mayonnaise
4 oz. Roquefort cheese,
crumbled

1/2 tsp. garlic salt
7/8 c. buttermilk

Mix all ingredients in a jar, shake well, and refrigerate 6 hours prior to using. Will keep several weeks.

Nutty Fruit Dressing

1 (7 oz.) jar marshmallow cream
1 c. salted peanuts, coarsely
chopped

1/3 c. pineapple juice
2 tsp. lemon juice

Combine marshmallow cream, lemon juice, and pineapple juice; mix well. Stir in peanuts. Chill well. Stir before serving. Serve over assorted fresh fruit. Yield: 1-1/3 cups.

Lettuce Salad

7 c. torn leaf lettuce
1/4 c. butter or margarine
1/4 tsp. salt

1 bunch green onions, sliced
1/4 c. vinegar

Combine lettuce and green onions in a large bowl; set aside. Combine butter and remaining ingredients in a saucepan; bring to a boil. Pour over lettuce; toss gently. Serve immediately. Yield: 6 to 8 servings.

Chicken Salad

2 c. chicken
1 c. celery

Miracle Whip
3 hard-boiled eggs

Chop chicken, and while still warm, add Miracle Whip to moisten. When cool, add chopped celery and chopped eggs. Then add mayonnaise as needed. Serve in lettuce cup.

Frozen Banana Salad

1 c. sour cream
1 lg. can crushed pineapple
    with liquid

2 mashed bananas
1 c. sugar

Mix together and freeze.

Cucumber Salad

2 lg. cucumbers, peeled and
    thinly sliced
2 tsp. salt
1 c. sour cream

2 tbsp. vinegar
1/4 tsp. pepper
1 lg. onion, thinly sliced

Sprinkle cucumbers with salt and let stand in refrigerator for several hours. Rinse in cold water to remove salt. Blend sour cream, vinegar, and pepper. Add cucumbers and onions to mixture. Return to refrigerator. Serves 6.

Cranberry Salad

1 pkg. orange-pineapple gelatin
1/2 jar cranberry-orange relish
1 lg. can crushed pineapple
1/2 c. chopped nuts

Dissolve gelatin in 1 cup boiling water. Add cranberry-orange relish, pineapple, and nuts. Chill. Serves 8.

Cranberry Salad

1 (1 lb.) can whole cranberry
   sauce
1/2 c. sugar
1 (large) crushed pineapple
2 (3 oz.) boxes cherry Jell-O
2 c. hot water

Dissolve the Jell-O in boiling water. Add the rest of ingredients. Turn into a mold and chill until firm.

Frozen Strawberry Salad

1 can Eagle Brand milk
1 can crushed pineapple,
   drained
1 can strawberry pie filling
1 Cool Whip

Mix together with mixer, blending well. Pour into baking dish and freeze.

Carrot Pineapple Salad

2 c. grated carrots
1 sm. can crushed pineapple
   in juice
1 tbsp. mayonnaise
2 pkg. sweetener or sugar to
   taste

Mix all ingredients well and serve chilled.

Orange Cottage Cheese Dressing
1 c. (8 oz.) cream cheese
1/4 c. frozen concentrated
   orange juice, thawed,
   undiluted

1 tsp. sugar
1/4 tsp. ginger
Dash salt

Put all ingredients into blender. Cover and process at high speed until smooth and creamy. Yield: 1 cup. Very good on fruit salad.

Vegetable Salad
1 pkg. frozen mixed vegetables
4 stalks celery, diced
1 onion, diced

1 can kidney beans, drained
   and rinsed

Cook mixed vegetables 10 minutes, cool, and add other ingredients. Can be eaten plain or with your favorite dressing.

Mandarin Orange Salad
1 med. carton Cool Whip
1 can mandarin orange slices,
   drained

1 sm. carton cottage cheese
1 pkg. (3 oz.) orange Jell-O

Mix together all ingredients and mold. Delicious as a salad or dessert. Serves 6.

Sweet Sauce for Egg Rolls
2 (12 oz.) jars apple jelly
1 (5 oz.) jar horseradish,
   drained

1 (9 oz.) jar pineapple sauce
1 (5 oz.) jar Mr. Mustard

Mix all ingredients in blender and refrigerate. Serve with egg rolls.

Hollandaise Sauce

3 egg yolks
1/2 c. firm butter, cut into
    eighths

1/4 tsp. salt
2 tbsp. lemon juice

In small heavy saucepan, stir yolks, juice and salt briskly over low heat. Add half the butter; stir over very low heat until butter is melted. Add remaining butter, stirring briskly until butter is melted and sauce thickens. (Butter should melt slowly to give eggs time to cook and thicken sauce without curdling.) Serve hot or at room temperature. Refrigerate if not using immediately. **NOTE:** Leftover sauce can be stored covered in refrigerator for several days. Before serving stir in small amount of hot water.

Double Boiler Hollandaise Sauce

3 egg yolks
2 tbsp. lemon juice
1/2 tsp. salt

1/2 c. butter, melted
1/2 c. water, boiling

Combine egg yolks, lemon juice, salt and butter in blender. Blend until smooth or about 5 seconds. Remove cover and gradually add boiling water. Pour all in top of double boiler and cook until sauce is like soft custard. Remove double boiler from heat and serve warm. This hollandaise sauce will keep for days in refrigerator and can be reheated. Yield: 1 cup.

Cranberry Sauce Mold

1 pkg. black cherry gelatin
3/4 c. hot water

1 lb. whole cranberry sauce
1/4 c. ginger ale

Dissolve gelatin in hot water. Stir in cranberry sauce and ginger ale. Pour into greased small mold. Chill several hours. Serves 4-6.

Classic Hollandaise Sauce

3 egg yolks
Dash of red pepper
1/2 c. butter or margarine

1/8 tsp. salt
2 tbsp. lemon juice

Beat egg yolks, salt and red pepper in top of a double boiler; gradually add lemon juice, stirring constantly. Add about one-third of butter to egg mixture; cook over hot, not boiling, water, stirring constantly, until butter melts. Add another third of butter, stirring constantly. As sauce thickens, stir in remaining butter. Cook until thickened. Yield: about 3/4 cup.

Blender variation: Use the same ingredients and amounts as for Classic Hollandaise Sauce. Place egg yolks, salt, red pepper, and lemon juice in container of an electric blender. Cover and blend at high speed about 5 seconds. Melt butter in a small saucepan. With blender on high, gradually add melted butter to egg mixture in a slow, steady stream. Blend about 30 seconds or until sauce is thickened. Yield: about 3/4 cup.

Mixer Hollandaise Sauce

6 egg yolks
2 tbsp. lemon juice

1 tbsp. dry white wine
1-1/2 c. butter, melted

Combine egg yolks, wine, and lemon juice in top of a double boiler. Place over boiling water, and cook, beating at medium speed of an electric mixer, 3 minutes or until thickened. Remove from heat. Add butter, 1 tablespoon at a time, beating at medium speed of an electric mixer until thickened. Yield: 2 cups.

Lemon Sauce for Gingerbread

1 c. sugar
1/2 c. butter
1 egg

1 lemon, juice and grated rind
3 tbsp. boiling water

Mix all ingredients in top of double boiler and cook until thick. Serve hot on gingerbread. Will keep in refrigerator and can be reheated. Yield: 1 cup.

Currant Sauce for Game

8 oz. currant jelly
2 tbsp. brandy

1/2 c. fresh mint leaves or
1/4 c. dried mint leaves

Melt jelly with brandy. When warm and smooth, add mint leaves. Serve over hot game. Yield: 1 cup.

Mike's Homemade Pickles

1 gal. dill pickles

5 lb. bag sugar

Drain juice off of pickles. Slice pickles 1/2'' thick. Arrange pickles in jar, in layers with sugar. Let stand in refrigator for at least 3 days, shaking occasionally.

Orange Sauce for Angel Food Cake

4 egg yolks, beaten
Juice and rind of 2 sm. or 1
   lg. orange

1/2 pt. heavy cream, whipped
2/3 c. sugar

Cook egg yolks, sugar, juice and rind of orange in top of double boiler until it begins to thicken. Place in refrigerator. One hour before using sauce, add whipped cream.

Lamb Sauce

4 tbsp. butter
2 tbsp. lemon juice
2 tbsp. wine vinegar

1/2 tsp. black pepper
1/2 tsp. red pepper

Combine all ingredients; heat until blended. Serve in sauce boat over lamb.

Tartar Sauce

2 tsp. capers
3 tbsp. mayonnaise

1/4 tsp. onion juice
5 drops lemon juice

Crush capers and mix all ingredients. May be kept in small tightly covered jar in refrigerator for a few days. Excellent on scallops, shrimp, crabmeat, & other seafood.

Hot Fudge Sauce

5 squares unsweetened chocolate
1/2 c. butter

3 c. confectioners sugar
1 can evaporated milk

Melt chocolate and butter; remove from heat. Mix in sugar and milk alternately. Bring to boil over medium heat, stirring constantly. Cook and stir 8 minutes or until thick. Serve warm. Yield: 3 cups. Can be stored in refrigerator and reheated.

Chocolate Fudge Sauce

7 oz. unsweetened chocolate
1 tbsp. butter or margarine
1 (12 oz.) can evaporated milk

1-3/4 c. sugar
1/4 tsp. salt

In double boiler melt chocolate; add sugar, butter, and salt, stirring until well blended. Add evaporated milk; cook until thick. Remove from heat. Serve warm. **MICRONOTE:** Place all ingredients in large glass bowl. Cook on HIGH 3-1/2 to 4 minutes, or until thick, stirring every minute. Yield: 4 cups.

Horseradish Sauce

1 (8 oz.) carton commercial
  sour cream

2 tbsp. milk
1-1/2 tbsp. prepared horseradish

Combine all ingredients; stir well. Yield: 1 cup. Excellent served on roast beef, prime ribs or steaks.

Creamy Chocolate Sauce

1 (6 oz.) pkg. semisweet
   chocolate morsels
1/2 tsp. vanilla extract

1/2 c. half-and-half
1 c. marshmallow cream

Combine chocolate morsels and half-and-half in a 1-quart glass measure; microwave at HIGH 2 minutes or until chocolate is almost melted, stirring after 1 minute. Stir until smooth. Spoon marshmallow cream into chocolate mixture; microwave at HIGH 45 seconds to 1 minute or until marshmallow cream softens. Add vanilla; stir with a wire whisk until smooth. Serve warm over ice cream or pound cake. Yield: 2 cups.

Marinade for Chicken

1 part sherry
1 part pineapple juice

2 parts soy sauce
Garlic to taste

Marinate chicken overnight, then charcoal chicken.

Cream Gravy

1/4 c. pan drippings
2-1/2 to 3 c. hot milk
1/8 to 1/4 tsp. pepper

1/4 c. all-purpose flour
1/2 tsp. salt

Pour off all except 1/4 cup drippings from skillet in which chicken or other meat was fried; place skillet over medium heat. Add flour, and stir until browned. Gradually add hot milk; cook, stirring constantly, until thickened and bubbly. Stir in salt and pepper. Serve hot. Yield: 2-3/4 cups.

Blender Mayonnaise

1 egg
1 c. oil, divided
2 tbsp. lemon juice

1/2 tsp. salt
Dash Tabasco

Drop egg into blender. Add 1/4 cup oil and rest of ingredients in the order given (except 3/4 cup oil). Turn on blender to a middle speed and pour remaining oil in finest possible steady stream. If oil pools on top of mayonnaise, cut off blender and run spatula down inside of blender to release air pocket. Then resume the mayonnaise making. Several batches of mayonnaise may be made at the same time without cleaning the blender between each one.

Slaw

4 c. cabbage
1 c. pickle relish, drained

1/2 c. mayonnaise
1/3 c. sugar

Shred cabbage and mix with all ingredients. Refrigerate before serving.

Slaw Stuffed Tomatoes

Tomatoes
Finely cut slaw

Salt to taste
Sweet pickle

Select a tomato for each person to be served. Skin and remove seed and pulp. Salt lightly, and fill with finely cut slaw. Garnish top with chopped sweet pickle. Chill.

Marinated Vegetables

Cherry tomatoes
Broccoli flowerets

Italian dressing
Cauliflower

Wash vegetables, chop slightly, and marinate in Zesty Italian dressing for about 4 hours. Drain before serving.

Cranberry Sauce

1 (12-16 oz.) pkg. fresh
  cranberries
1-1/2 c. sugar

1/4 c. water or unsweetened
  orange juice

Combine all ingredients in a 1-1/2-quart covered casserole. Micro-wave on 100% power for 8 minutes or until cranberries pop. Stir once. Let stand 5-6 minutes. Refrigerate.

Quick Slaw

1 bag slaw mix from produce
  dept. of grocery store

1 bottle Kraft slaw dressing
1 tsp. celery seed

Toss together and chill a couple of hours before serving.

Vegetables

Macaroni Pie

2 c. cooked macaroni, (1 c.
    uncooked)
2-1/2 c. sharp cheddar cheese,
    grated

5 eggs beaten
Approximately 1-1/2 c. milk
1/2 tsp. salt

Grease a 2-quart casserole and put alternate layers of cooked macaroni and grated cheese, ending with cheese on top. Add enough milk to the beaten eggs so that the pie will be covered. The salt should be put into the egg and milk mixture. Bake at 375° for about 40 minutes or until firm in the center. Serves about 10.

Crab Rice

1 lb. bacon, cooked and
    drained
1 lb. crabmeat, lump or claw

1 c. onion, diced
3 c. cooked rice
Salt and pepper to taste

Crumble bacon and mix with crabmeat, onion and rice. Add salt and pepper to taste. Pour into casserole. Bake 25 to 30 minutes in 350° oven. Serve with tossed salad and garlic bread. Serves 6 to 8.

Red Rice

2 onions, chopped
1 c. bacon drippings
2-1/2 c. rice, raw

1 (15 oz.) can tomato sauce
10 oz. water
Salt and pepper to taste

Cook onions in bacon drippings until tender. Add tomato sauce and water. Add salt and pepper to taste; cook 15 minutes. Rinse rice and drain off as much water as possible. Add rice and tomato sauce mixture together. Put in rice steamer. Steam hard for 1 hour before opening. Open and mix rice in sauce that settled on top. Serves 6.

Baked Rice

1 stick butter
1 med. onion, chopped
2 cans beef consomme

1 c. uncooked rice
1 can mushrooms (optional)

Saute onion in butter until tender. Combine other ingredients and pour into large casserole. Cover and bake at 350° for 1 hour. Serves 6.

Brown Rice

1 c. uncooked rice
1 can water
1 envelope dry onion soup mix

1 can beef consomme
1 stick margarine

Mix ingredients together in 2-quart casserole dish with lid. Bake covered at 350° for 1 hour.

Twice Baked Potatoes

8 to 10 med. sized potatoes
1 c. sour cream
1 c. grated cheddar cheese

1 egg
Salt
Paprika (Optional)

Bake potatoes in 350° oven for 1 hour. Do not wrap in foil. When done, cut in half and scoop out inside. With mixer, whip potatoes and add sour cream. Then add egg and salt to taste. Last, add cheese. You do not want cheese to melt when you add it at this point. Fill halves with potato mixture and sprinkle tops with paprika. Put on tray and freeze. When frozen you can drop them into a plastic bag and return to freezer. To reheat, bake at 350° for 30 minutes.

Nutty Potatoes

12 med. potatoes
2 onions
1 qt. half-and-half

1 tsp. salt
1/4 tsp. pepper
1/8 lb. butter

Grind potatoes and 2 onions into one quart half-and-half. Add salt, pepper and butter. Put in casserole and bake 325° for 4 hours. Stir occasionally. Serves 12.

New Potatoes With Mustard Sauce

Water
8 sm. new potatoes, about
 1-1/2 lb.

2 tbsp. prepared mustard
2 tbsp. sugar or to taste
1 c. (8 oz.) sour cream

In medium saucepan bring 1 inch water and potatoes to boil. Cover and cook over medium heat 20 minutes or until tender. Meantime mix sour cream, mustard and sugar until well blended. Drain potatoes, top with mustard sauce. Makes 4 servings.

New Potatoes

15 to 20 sm. new potatoes
1 stick melted butter
Flour

Salt
Pepper

Boil potatoes until done. Slip off skins. Roll in melted butter. Roll in flour seasoned with salt and pepper. Roll again in butter, just enough to wet flour. Place on cookie sheet and bake at 400° for 15 minutes until slightly brown and crusty.

Puffed Potatoes

Sm. new potatoes
Vegetable oil

Salt

Wash and dry the potatoes. Rub the skins with vegetable oil. Cut each potato in half lengthwise; salt the cut surfaces. Bake in 450° oven until browned and puffed, about 10 minutes.

Dressed-Up Potatoes

4 lg. baking potatoes
1/2 to 3/4 c. Wish-Bone
    Creamy Bell Pepper or
    Creamy Cucumber Dressing

1 c. shredded cheddar cheese
1 c. cubed, cooked ham

Preheat oven to 400°. Bake potatoes until done. Scoop potato from shells, saving shells. In medium bowl, mash potatoes with either dressing; stir in cheese and ham. Refill shells. Bake 15 minutes or until heated through. Makes 4 servings.

Fluffy Potatoes

6 potatoes, boiled and peeled
2 (3 oz.) pkg. cream cheese
1 c. sour cream

4 tbsp. margarine
Salt and pepper

Beat potatoes until fluffy and add rest of ingredients. Pour into greased casserole. Dot with margarine. Bake at 350° for 30 minutes. Serves 6.

Charcoal Potatoes

6 med. potatoes
3 (.25 oz.) envelopes instant
    onion soup mix

1/2 c. + 2 tbsp. butter or
    margarine, softened

Scrub potatoes; do not peel. Slice lengthwise into 1/2-inch slices. Arrange slices of each potato on a square of heavy-duty aluminum foil to make individual bundles. Combine butter and soup mix, mixing well. Divide mixture evenly, and spread on each potato. Fold foil edges over, and wrap securely. Grill over medium-hot coals 50 to 60 minutes, turning once. Yield: 6 servings.

Marinated Asparagus Spears

2 lb. fresh asparagus
1/2 c. cider vinegar
1 tsp. salt

1/2 c. sugar
1-1/2 tbsp. lemon juice
1/8 tsp. pepper

Cut off tough ends of asparagus. Cook asparagus, covered, in boiling water 6 to 8 minutes; drain, reserving 1/2 cup liquid. Place asparagus in a large container; set aside. Combine reserved 1/2 cup asparagus liquid and remaining ingredients in a small saucepan; stir well. Bring to a boil, stirring constantly; pour over asparagus. Cover; chill 8 hours. Yield: 8 servings.

Grilled Onions

4 med. onions
Salt and pepper to taste

4 tbsp. butter
4 slices bacon, cut in half

Peel onions, removing a thin slice from top and bottom. Make a crisscross, cut 3/4 of the way through onions. Sprinkle on salt and pepper. Dab 1 tablespoon butter in center of each onion. Lay two pieces of bacon across top. Wrap each onion in foil and grill over medium hot coals for 45 minutes or until tender.

Apple Carrots

1 can fingerling carrots
1 can apple pie filling

1/4 stick margarine
1/2 c. brown sugar

Empty carrots into bottom of casserole dish. Spread apple pie filling on top of carrots. Add brown sugar and pats of butter. Bake at 350° for about 45 minutes.

Pickled Beets

1 can sliced beets
1 med. onion (sliced)

1 c. sugar
1 c. white vinegar

Combine sugar and vinegar in a saucepan. Bring to a boil and stir. Pour over sliced beets and onions. Cool, then cover and store in refrigerator overnight before serving.

Artichoke Hearts

4 tbsp. butter
2 oz. bleu cheese

2 (14 oz.) can artichoke hearts, well drained

Melt butter and cheese together over low heat. Cut artichokes into bite size pieces. Add to cheese mixture. Serve in chafing dish. Serves 12.

Mushroom Casserole

1 lb. fresh mushrooms, sliced
2 c. French bread, cubed
1/3 c. dry white wine

1/2 c. butter, melted
Salt and pepper

Butter 2-quart round casserole. Layer 1/3 mushrooms, 1/3 bread and spoon on 1/3 melted butter. Sprinkle with salt and pepper. Repeat process. Pour wine evenly over casserole. Cover and bake at 325° for 25 minutes. Uncover and continue baking until brown. Serves 6.

Okra Pilau

2 c. raw rice
2 tsp. salt
8 slices bacon, cut into 4 or 5
   pieces each

1 onion, chopped
2 lb. okra, sliced crosswise
2 c. water

Put rice, salt and water in rice steamer. Cook bacon and onion in skillet for 5-8 minutes. Add okra to bacon and onion and cook until okra browns on edges. When all of water has been absorbed by rice, add okra mixture and mix thoroughly. Add more salt if needed. Let mixture cook 20-30 minutes. Serves 8-10.

Parmesan Zucchini

4 or 5 sm. zucchini, quartered
   and sliced in 2-in. lengths
Salt

Pepper
1/4 c. Parmesan cheese
2 tbsp. butter

Drop zucchini into boiling water. Reduce heat to simmer and cook 5 to 10 minutes. Do not overcook. Drain and run under cold water. Butter a shallow baking dish and arrange zucchini in 1 layer. Sprinkle with salt, pepper and Parmesan cheese. Dribble butter over top. Cook under broiler until zucchini is hot and golden. Serves 6.

Scalloped Tomatoes

1-1/2 c. herb stuffing cumbs
5-1/3 tbsp. butter, melted
1 (14-1/2 oz.) can whole
   tomatoes

1/4 c. brown sugar
1/2 tsp. salt

Put stuffing crumbs into a 1-quart baking dish. Pour butter over the crumbs and toss to coat. Mix the juice from tomatoes with brown sugar and salt. Nest the tomatoes down in the bread crumbs and pour the juice mixture over the top. Bake at 425° for 25 to 30 minutes. Serves 4.

Baked Cherry Tomatoes

24 cherry tomatoes
4 tbsp. butter
1 tsp. sugar

Dash salt
Fresh parsley, chopped

Slice tomatoes almost through and place in baking dish. Add butter, salt and sugar. Bake in 350° oven for 8 to 10 minutes. Shake the pan occasionally so the tomatoes turn in the butter. Sprinkle parsley on top when done. Serves 4 as an accompaniment.

Spinach Casserole

2 pkg. frozen spinach
1 can cream of mushroom soup

8 oz. pkg. cream cheese
1 can French fried onion rings

Cook spinach according to package directions and drain well. Cut cream cheese into chunks and add to spinach. Stir until cream cheese is melted. Add mushroom soup to spinach mixture. Fold in 3/4 can of onion rings. Place mixture in casserole dish and bake in 350° oven for 25 minutes. Top casserole with remaining onions and bake 5 minutes more. (Green beans can be substituted for the spinach.)

Tomato Rice

1/4 lb. bacon, diced
1 onion, chopped
1 c. uncooked rice

1 (1 lb.) can tomatoes with
   juice
1/2 c. water

Saute bacon and onion until bacon is browned. Add rice and stir until rice is lightly browned. Stir in tomatoes and water and bring to a boil. Cover and simmer on low heat 30 minutes. Add water if rice seems too dry or if barbecue chef is slow. Serves 8.

Peas and Snow Peas

2 (10 oz.) pkg. frozen tender
    tiny peas
1 (6 oz.) pkg. frozen snow pea
    pods

2 tbsp. butter or margarine,
    melted
1/2 tsp. dried whole dillweed
1/4 tsp. salt

Saute tiny peas in butter in a large skillet 5 minutes, stirring occasionally. Add snow pea pods, and cook over medium heat 5 minutes, stirring occasionally. Stir in dillweed and salt, and cook mixture 2 minutes. Transfer to serving bowl. Yield: 8 servings.

Asparagus Caesar

3 lb. fresh asparagus spears
1/4 c. + 2 tbsp. lemon juice
1/4 c. + 2 tbsp. grated
    Parmesan cheese

1/4 c. + 2 tbsp. butter or
    margarine, melted

Snap off tough ends of asparagus; remove scales with a knife or vegetable peeler, if desired. Cook asparagus, covered, in a small amount of boiling water 6 to 8 minutes or until crisp-tender. Drain. Place asparagus in a 12 x 8 x 2-inch baking dish. Combine butter and lemon juice; pour over asparagus. Sprinkle cheese over asparagus. Place under broiler until browned. Yield: 12 servings.

Stuffed Mushrooms

1 lb. fresh mushrooms
8 oz. Swiss cheese
1 c. herb stuffing

3/4 stick margarine
1 tsp. salt

Clean mushrooms and slightly broil in oven. Mix together and make balls of stuffing mixture and stuff mushrooms. Broil until slightly brown. Crab meat can be added to this mixture.

Cranberry Pears

3 fresh pears
2 (6 oz.) cans water
1 c. sugar, divided

1 (6 oz.) can frozen lemonade
  concentrate
2 c. fresh cranberries

Peel, halve, and core pears. Combine lemonade concentrate, water, and 1/2 cup sugar in skillet. Add pears; simmer, covered, until pears are almost tender; add cranberries and 1/2 cup sugar. Simmer 5-10 minutes more, until cranberries are tender. Chill. Remove pears onto serving plate with slotted spoon; spoon some of cranberries into each pear half. **MICRONOTE:** Place lemonade, water, 1/2 cup sugar, and pears in glass bowl. Bring to boil on HIGH; cook on MEDIUM 5 minutes. Add cranberries and 1/2 cup sugar. Bring to boil on HIGH; cook on MEDIUM 2-3 minutes. Continue as above. Serves 6.

Onion Rings

3 lg. onions, sliced and
  separated into rings
1 to 1-1/2 c. club soda

2 c. packaged extra-light
  pancake mix
Oil

Blend pancake mix with club soda according to preference (less soda for thickly battered rings). Dip rings into batter. Fry in hot oil until golden. Drain on absorbent toweling; serve at once. (Leftover onion rings may be frozen in single layer on cookie sheet. When frozen, place in plastic bag. Reheat in oven on cookie sheet.) Serves 6-8.

Parmesan Corn on the Cob

4 ears fresh corn
1/4 c. grated Parmesan cheese
1/4 tsp. dried whole salad herbs

1/4 c. butter or margarine,
  softened

Remove husks and silks from corn just before cooking. Combine butter and remaining ingredients, stirring well. Spread mixture on corn, and place each ear on a piece of heavy-duty plastic wrap. Roll wrap length-wise around each ear, and twist wrap at each end. Arrange ears of corn, spoke-fashion, on a microwave-safe glass plate. Microwave corn at HIGH 10 to 13 minutes, rearranging ears occasionally.

Asparagus With Cashew Sauce

2 (10 oz.) pkg. frozen asparagus
    or 1 lb. fresh asparagus
4 tsp. lemon juice
1/2 c. salted cashew nuts
1/2 c. melted butter

Cook asparagus. Combine all other ingredients and cook over low heat for five minutes. Pour over asparagus and serve hot.

Brussels Sprouts

1/2 c. water
1 (10 oz.) pkg. frozen brussels
    sprouts
1 chicken-flavored bouillon cube
1/2 c. chopped onion
2 tbsp. tarragon vinegar

Place water in a medium saucepan; bring to a boil. Add bouillon cube, stirring until dissolved. Add brussels sprouts; return to a boil. Cover, reduce heat, and simmer 5 to 6 minutes or until brussels sprouts are tender. Drain. Add chopped onion and tarragon vinegar to brussels sprouts; stir gently. Cover brussels sprouts, and chill 3 to 4 hours, stirring occasionally. Yield: 4 servings.

Italian-Style Broccoli

1-1/2 lb. fresh broccoli
2 cloves garlic, minced
1/4 c. olive oil
2 tbsp. lemon juice

Trim off large leaves of broccoli. Remove tough ends of lower stalks, and wash broccoli thoroughly. Cut broccoli into flowerets. Cook broccoli in a large skillet, covered, in a small amount of boiling water 5 minutes or until crisp-tender; drain in colander. Pour oil into skillet; add garlic, and cook over medium high heat, stirring constantly, until bubbly. Add broccoli and lemon juice; toss gently. Cover and cook 1 minute. Remove from heat, and arrange broccoli on a serving platter. Serve immediately. Yield: 6 servings.

Hopping John

1 c. dried field peas
4 c. water
2 tsp. salt

1/3 lb. bacon
1 lge. onion, chopped
1 c. rice, uncooked and washed

Boil peas in water and salt until tender. Fry bacon until crisp. Remove from pan and crumble. Pour off half the grease and cook onion until tender. Combine peas, 1-1/2 cups pea liquid, rice, bacon and onion. Put in rice steamer and cook until done or about 1 hour. Remove top from steamer the last 10 to 15 minutes of cooking time and fluff. Serves 6.

Tallulah's Sweet Potato Surprise

1 lb. can sweet potatoes
Lg. marshmallows
Corn flakes

1 sm. can crushed pineapple,
    drained well

Mash sweet potatoes. Mix crushed pineapple with potatoes. Take large marshmallow and put sweet potato mixture around it. Then roll in corn flakes. (This is very messy, but worth it). Place balls in lightly greased casserole. Bake 30 minutes at 350° degrees.

Main Dishes

Crepes

6 eggs
1 c. milk
6 tbsp. melted butter

1 c. water
1-1/2 c. flour

Mix all ingredients together. Fry 1/4 cup of batter in omelet pan until light brown. Remove from pan and put between paper towels. Freeze. To make filling use any kind of cream soup and meat. For desserts use pie filling and sprinkle with powdered sugar. You can top with sour cream or whipped topping.

Basic Processor Crepes

1-1/2 c. all-purpose flour
2 tbsp. butter or margarine,
    chilled

1/4 tsp. salt
3 eggs
2 c. milk

Position knife blade in food processor bowl. Place flour, salt, and butter in processor bowl. Top with cover, and process until mixture resembles coarse meal. Add eggs through food chute, one at a time, processing just until blended. With processor running, pour milk through food chute, and process until smooth. Refrigerate batter 1 to 2 hours. (This allows flour particles to swell and soften so the crepes will be light in texture.) Brush bottom of a 6- or 8-inch crepe pan or heavy skillet with oil; place the pan over medium heat just until hot, not smoking. Pour 2 to 3 tablespoons batter into pan; quickly tilt pan in all directions so batter covers pan in a thin film. Cook about 1 minute or until lightly browned. Lift edge of crepe to test for doneness. Crepe is ready for flipping when it can be shaken loose from pan. Flip crepe, and cook about 30 seconds on other side. (This side is usually spotty brown and is the side on which the filling is placed.) Repeat until all batter is used. Place crepes on a towel to cool. Stack between layers of wax paper to prevent sticking. Yield: 24 (6-inch) crepes or 18 (8-inch) crepes.

Omelet

4 eggs, separated
2 tbsp. flour
2 tbsp. butter

3/4 c. milk
Salt and pepper

Add flour, butter, salt, pepper and milk to beaten egg yolks. Fold in stiffly beaten egg whites. Pour in greased iron frying pan or omelet pan and cook on top of stove over moderate heat for a few minutes. Cook in 400° oven until done.

Sauce: Fry 2 slices bacon. Remove from frying pan. Cook 1 small chopped onion, 2 stalks chopped celery, and 1 chopped green pepper in bacon drippings until tender. Add 1 16-oz. can of tomatoes, crumbled bacon and salt and pepper. Cook until it thickens. Pour half of sauce in middle of basic omelet. Fold omelet over and pour remainder of sauce on top. Serves 4.

Mushroom Filling for Omelet

6 lg. mushrooms, sliced
3 med. green onions, thinly
  sliced, tops and all

1-1/2 tbsp. sour cream
Salt and pepper
2 tbsp. butter

Saute mushrooms and onions in butter only until mushrooms start to change color. Add sour cream, salt and pepper. As soon as mixture is hot remove from heat and spoon onto omelet. Fold over and serve. Serves 2.

Cheese Souffle

2 eggs, beaten
1-1/4 c. milk
2 c. sharp cheddar cheese,
  coarsely grated

6 saltine crackers, coarsely
  crushed
Dash salt and pepper

Combine eggs with milk and seasonings. Add cheese and saltine crackers. Put in lightly greased 1-quart casserole. Bake in 375° oven for 40-45 minutes. Serve with crisp bacon and toast. Serves 3.

Microwave No Crust Quiche

1-1/2 c. shredded Swiss cheese
4-5 med. eggs
1 tall can (13 oz.) evaporated
  milk
3/4 tsp. salt
1/4 tsp. sugar
Dash pepper

Sprinkle cheese in 9- or 10-inch glass pie plate or square casserole dish. Combine remaining ingredients and beat till well blended. Pour over cheese. Bake 4 minutes, turn dish 1/4 turn. Bake another 4 minutes and turn. Bake another 4 minutes and let set 10-15 minutes to finish cooking. **Variations:** Use bacon, ham, chicken, turkey with 1/4 cup minced onion. Mix with cheese in bottom of dish. Use 2 packages (10 oz.) chopped broccoli or spinach.

Spaghetti Sauce

1 lb. ground beef
8 oz. can tomato sauce
1-1/2 tomato sauce cans of
  water
2 envelopes Lawry's spaghetti
  sauce mix
6 oz. can tomato paste
1-1/2 c. water

Brown beef and drain. Combine the remaining ingredients and simmer at least 30 minutes. Serve over noodles. This sauce freezes great! I have used this recipe for years and my children like it better than any of the many other ones that I have tried on them!

Honey Chicken

1 (3 lb.) chicken, cut up
4 tbsp. butter
1/2 c. honey
1/4 c. prepared mustard
1 tsp. salt

Wash chicken pieces; pat dry. Melt butter in oblong baking dish. Combine other ingredients and add to baking dish. Roll chicken in mixture to coat on both sides. Then arrange in single layer. Bake at 375° for 1 hour or until chicken is tender and glazed.

Savannah Chicken

1 fryer (cut up)
Salad dressing (Miracle Whip)
3/4 c. cornflakes

3 tbsp. sesame seeds
Salt
Pepper

Coat chicken with salad dressing. Dip chicken into crumbs and seeds that have been mixed together. Salt and pepper each piece of chicken. Place chicken in baking dish. Bake 350° oven for 1 hour.

Low Cholesterol Savannah Chicken

1 chicken, cut in pieces
3/4 c. cornflakes
Salt and pepper

1 c. yogurt
3 tbsp. sesame seeds

Coat chicken with yogurt. Dip chicken into crumbs and seeds that have been mixed together. Salt and pepper each piece of chicken. Place chicken in baking dish. Bake at 350° for 1 hour.

Chicken Casserole

1 carton (1/2 pt.) sour cream
1 can cream of mushroom soup

8-10 chicken breasts
Bacon

Mix undiluted soup and sour cream. Spread over chicken in oblong dish. Place strips of bacon over each piece of chicken. Bake (uncovered) 300° for 3 hours. Do not salt chicken.

Italian Boneless Chicken

8 boneless chicken breasts
1 c. grated mozarella cheese

1 lg. jar Ragu spaghetti
  sauce, any flavor

Place chicken in bottom of oblong casserole in one layer. Salt and pepper. Pour jar of Ragu sauce over chicken until chicken is covered. Bake at 350° for 45 minutes or until done. Sprinkle cheese over top. Return to oven and bake until cheese melts. Serve on spaghetti if desired.

Chicken/Broccoli Casserole

1 box frozen chopped broccoli (thawed)
1 (7 oz.) can chicken (or 2 5-oz. size)
1 can cream of mushroom soup (undiluted)
1 c. cooked rice

Mix soup, chicken and rice; fold in broccoli. Bake in 350° oven till hot (30-40 minutes).

Waverly Baked Chicken

1 cut-up fryer (2-3 lb.)
1 pkg. Waverly crackers, crushed
1 stick margarine
1 egg, beaten
1 tsp. salt

Use an oblong casserole for this recipe. Salt chicken pieces. Beat egg and leave in large bowl. Dip chicken pieces in egg, then roll in cracker crumbs and place in casserole. Melt stick of margarine. After all chicken is in casserole, pour melted butter over chicken. Cover pan very tightly with foil. Bake in 325° oven for 2 hours.

Chicken Casserole

8 chicken breasts
8 oz. sour cream
1 roll Ritz crackers
2 cans cream of chicken soup

Mix soup with sour cream. Pour over chicken. Crush crackers and spread on top. Bake at 350° for 1 hour.

Chicken Bake With Cheese

6 to 8 chicken breast halves or cut-up whole chicken
1 can cream of mushroom soup
1 can cream of celery soup
1 c. grated sharp cheese

Place chicken in baking pan. Mix the soups (undiluted) and cheese well and pour over chicken making sure that chicken is covered. (Mixture is thick.) Bake at 350° until chicken is tender. This makes a delicious gravy to serve over rice with chicken. Serves 6.

Baked Chicken

1 broiler, whole
Salt and pepper

Salt and pepper chicken inside and out. Place in brown paper bag. Place on cookie sheet in 350° oven for one hour, or until done.

Catalina Chicken

Catalina Kraft Salad Dressing, whole jar
1 pkg. Lipton onion soup
1 cut-up fryer
10 oz. jar apricot jelly or any kind you like

Mix all ingredients together and pour over chicken in casserole. Cook uncovered in a 300° oven for about 1-1/2 hours or until tender. Serves 4.

Oven-Fried Chicken

1/2 c. butter or margarine
Flour
Paprika
Lemon-pepper or pepper
4 chicken breast halves, skinned, or assorted chicken pieces
Salt or garlic salt

Melt butter in shallow baking dish. Dredge chicken pieces in flour; place meat down in butter. Sprinkle liberally with paprika, lemon-pepper, and garlic salt. Bake, uncovered, at 425° for 30 minutes. Turn chicken pieces; sprinkle again with seasonings. Bake 20 additional minutes. Serves 4.

Sweet and Sour Grilled Chicken

1 broiler-fryer chicken,
   cut into parts
2 tbsp. soy sauce

1/4 c. prepared yellow mustard
1/4 c. orange marmalade

Grill chicken pieces 4 inches above hot coals for 20 minutes, turning occasionally. Combine mustard, marmalade, and soy sauce; blend well. Brush over chicken. Grill additional 20-30 minutes, turning frequently and brushing with glaze. **MICRONOTE:** While coals are heating, cook chicken in shallow dish, covered, at MEDIUM for 20 minutes; turn once after 10 minutes. Remove to grill, brush with glaze, and continue as above for last 20-30 minutes of grilling time. Serves 4-6.

Lemon-Garlic Grilled Chicken

1 c. butter or margarine,
   melted
2 broiler-fryer chickens, halved
   or 8 chicken breast halves

1 c. lemon juice
2 (.7 oz) pkg. garlic salad
   dressing mix

Blend butter, lemon juice, and dressing mix. Refrigerate overnight. Place chicken on grill, skin-side up, 6 inches above grayed coals. Grill 1 hour, turning every 15 minutes. Meanwhile, heat sauce just until warm. Brush chicken generously with sauce; grill 30 minutes longer, brushing with sauce and turning every 2-3 minutes. To oven-broil, brush chicken with warmed sauce on all sides. Place skin-side down on broiler rack; set 7-8 inches from heat. Broil 15 minutes; turn. Brush with sauce; broil 15 additional minutes, brushing 1-2 times more, until richly browned. Test for doneness by making slit near hip joint; if juices are pink, broil additional 5 minutes or until juices run clear. Serves 4-8.

Beef Tenderloin With Crust

1 beef tenderloin
1 bag herb stuffing

1 bottle Italian dressing

Marinate tenderloin overnight in dressing. Next day, roll in herb stuffing. Bake at 500° for 15 minutes. Insert meat thermometer. Reduce temperature to 350° and bake until center is rare.

Durkee's Chicken

6 chicken breast halves
1/2 c. Durkee's Famous Sauce
3 c. cooked rice
1/2 c. butter, melted, or
1/2 c. oil

Place chicken breasts in single layer in shallow baking dish. Blend butter and Durkee's; pour over chicken. Bake, covered, at 350° for 45 minutes. Uncover; bake 15 minutes more or until brown. Serve chicken atop bed of rice; pour drippings over all. **MICRONOTE:** Blend butter and Durkee's; pour over chicken in shallow glass dish. Cover with waxed paper. Cook on HIGH 6 minutes per pound of chicken, turning dish several times. Serves 4-6.

Southern Fried Chicken

6 chicken breast halves or
   3-1/2 lb. assorted chicken
   pieces or 1 lb. chicken
   livers, halved
Salt
1 c. buttermilk
2 c. self-rising flour
1 tsp. lemon-pepper seasoning

Lightly salt chicken to taste. Place buttermilk in shallow dish and flour onto waxed paper. Dip each piece of chicken into buttermilk; sprinkle with lemon-pepper. Roll in flour, coating well; shake off any excess flour. Heat 2-inch depth of oil in large skillet to 350°. Place chicken, a few pieces at a time, in hot oil. (Take care to add extra chicken pieces slowly enough that oil temperature does not drop below 325°.) Cook until chicken is crisp and richly browned, turning once. Drain well on absorbent toweling. To keep hot, hold in warm oven. Serves 6.

Oven Fried Chicken

1 c. mayonnaise
6-8 boned chicken breasts
2 tbsp. mustard
Pepperidge Farm Herb
   Stuffing

Mix mayonnaise and mustard together. Dip chicken in mixture and roll in stuffing. Bake at 350° for 1 hour.

Beaumont Fried Chicken

1 (3-1/2 to 4 lb.) broiler-fryer,
   cut up
1/2 c. all-purpose flour
1 tsp. water

3/4 to 1 tsp. salt
1/4 to 1/2 tsp. pepper
3 to 3-1/2 c. shortening or
   lard

Rinse chicken; pat dry. Sprinkle with salt and pepper. Place flour in a plastic bag; place 2 or 3 pieces of chicken at a time into bag. Close securely, and shake until pieces are evenly coated. Heat shortening to 325° in a 10-inch iron skillet. Add chicken, and cook, uncovered, 25 to 30 minutes or until golden brown, turning once. Remove from heat; drain off fat. Return skillet to low heat; add water to chicken, cover, and allow chicken to steam 5 minutes. Yield: about 4 servings.

Crepes Au Salmon

12 crepes
1 c. sour cream, divided
1/2 lb. smoked salmon (lox),
   thinly sliced

12 tsp. fresh lemon juice
Coarse black pepper

Make 12 crepes or buy them from refrigerator section of grocery store. Spread sour cream on each crepe. Put thin strips of lox in middle of each crepe. Grind the pepper and add lemon juice. Roll up crepes and put in 9 x 13-inch Pyrex serving dish. Spread leftover sour cream on crepes. Place in 450° oven for 15 minutes before serving. Exquisite entree.

Fried Soft Shell Crabs

2 soft shell crabs
2 c. milk
2 tsp. salt

1/2 tsp. pepper
1/2 c. flour

Wash crab in cold water. Remove feathery substances, sand bag, and apron. Dry well. Combine milk, salt and pepper. Soak crab in seasoned milk for 15 minutes; roll in flour. Deep fat fry at 370° for 6 or 7 minutes. Serve with tartar sauce.

Low Country Boil

Bring a large pot of water 3/4 full to a boil. Put in 2-inch sections of smoked sausage and bring back to a boil. Add corn on the cob (niblets work best), and bring to a boil. Add shrimp (peeling and all) and bring to a boil. For added seasoning, you may place seafood boil in cheese cloth or a tea ball and place it in the water before it begins to boil. Also an onion may be cut up and cooked with this mixture too. Drain this mixture and serve buffet style.

PROPORTIONS: for 8 people
2-3 lb. smoked sausage   10 ears corn
2 lb. shrimp

These are approximate, so whatever ratios you use should be fine.

Shrimp-Stuffed Flounder

4 med. or 2 lge. flounder,   Salt and pepper to taste
  filleted   Lemon juice
1/2 c. butter or margarine,   1-1/2 lb. shrimp, cleaned,
  softened   deveined and split

Put half of the fillets in a shallow, aluminum foil-lined pan. Spread with 1/4 cup butter, then sprinkle on salt, pepper and lemon juice. Place shrimp on fish, then cover with the other half of the flounder. Sprinkle with salt, pepper and lemon juice and spread with remaining butter. Cover tightly with aluminum foil and bake 40 minutes at 400°. Serves 6.

White Clam Sauce for Linguine

1 tbsp. butter   3 (6-1/2 oz.) cans minced
2 cloves garlic, minced   clams, or 2 (10 oz.) cans
1 tbsp. flour   baby clams
Salt and white pepper to taste

Heat butter and gently saute garlic for 1 minute. Blend in flour. Add remaining ingredients; bring to simmer for 5 minutes, stirring often. Do not boil. Serve over hot cooked linguine or vermicelli. Serves 4.

Scalloped Oysters

1 qt. oysters, reserve liquor
Half-and-half
2 c. saltine cracker crumbs

2 tsp. pepper
2 tsp. salt
1 c. butter, melted

Add oyster liquor to half-and-half to make 1 pint. Heat. Mix saltine cracker crumbs, butter, pepper and salt. Layer the cracker crumb mixture in baking dish with oysters, beginning with crumbs and then oysters. Pour heated liquid over the top. Bake in preheated 375° oven for 20-30 minutes. Serves 6-8.

Beef Tenderloin

Beef tenderloin
1 c. red wine

1 c. soy sauce
1 c. olive oil

Marinate beef tenderloin in wine, soy sauce, and olive oil for 2 days, turning several times. Remove from marinade and cook uncovered in 500° oven for 40 minutes only. If using for cocktail party, figure 4 to 5 people per pound.

Onion Burgers

1 envelope Lipton Onion, Beefy
    Onion, or Beef Flavor
    Mushroom Soup Mix

1/2 c. water
2 lb. ground beef

In large bowl, combine all ingredients; mix thoroughly. Shape into 8 patties. Grill or broil until done. Top, if desired, with tomato. Makes 8 servings.

Eye of Round Roast

Round roast

Pepper or onion pepper

Garlic salt

Flour

Dampen the eye of round roast and coat with garlic salt and pepper or onion pepper. Roll in flour and put in a plastic bag. Refrigerate overnight (not necessary but better). The next day, roll the roast in flour again. Place roast on aluminum foil (uncovered) to hold juice. Bake 350° for 30 minutes per pound for rare. For well done, bake 45 minutes per pound.

Country Ham

Country ham

Water

Brown sugar

Cloves

Scrub country ham with brush and warm water. Line a roaster with extra strength heavy duty foil. Place ham on foil, fat side up. Place 1-1/2 cups water over ham and secure with foil tightly to retain juices. Bake at 350° for 20 to 25 minutes per pound. Let ham cool in foil and remove skin and fat carefully. When ham is cool, cover with brown sugar and cloves and run under broiler.

Roast Leg of Pork

7 to 9 lb. leg of fresh pork

Salt

1/2 c. onions, chopped

2 c. red wine

1/4 tsp. nutmeg

Preheat oven to 325°. Line roaster pan with aluminum foil. Put rack in roaster. Skin ham. Rub meat well with salt. Stuff crevices with onion; put any left over on top of meat. Put meat on rack in roaster with fat side up. Mix together the wine and nutmeg. Pour mixture into bottom of roaster. Ladle a few spoonfuls over the top of meat. Cover. Place in oven. Cook 20 to 25 minutes per pound. Baste every 15 to 20 minutes. Serves 10 to 12.

Roast Beef

1 (6 lb.) tenderloin
2 tsp. black pepper

6 slices bacon

Allow roast to stand at room temperature for 30 minutes. Place roast in open pan. Sprinkle with pepper. Arrange bacon slices on top, skewering with toothpicks. Put into 450° oven. Allow 10 minutes per pound for rare roast, 12 minutes per pound for medium. Remove from oven and allow to stand 15 minutes before carving. Serves 10.

Divine Beef Roast

1 clove garlic, crushed
1 c. soy sauce
1/4 c. bourbon

1 c. water
1 (6 lb.) roast (any cut)

Combine crushed garlic, soy sauce, bourbon, and water. Pour over roast and marinate for 24 hours in refrigerator. Charcoal 45 minutes on an open grill, or 30 to 35 minutes on a covered grill.

Drunken Roast

1 roast (rump or sirloin tip),
    approximately 4 lb.
1 (20 oz.) bottle tomato catsup

1 (12 oz.) can beer
1 lg. onion, sliced

Brown roast. Mix catsup, beer and onion. Add to roast. Simmer covered for 2 hours. Uncover and simmer for 1 more hour. Serves 6 to 8.

Beef Mushroom Casserole

2 lb. beef cubes
1 can cream of mushroom soup

1 can French onion soup
1/2 c. red wine

Mix together all ingredients in a casserole and bake at 350°, uncovered, for 3 hours. (Do not brown meat — just add raw meat to other ingredients.) Serve over rice. Serves 4 to 6. This can be frozen. NOTE: In last 30 minutes of baking you may add 1 can drained sliced mushrooms, or carrots, or small whole potatoes.

Fish With Wine and Cheese

1/2 c. butter
Salt, pepper and paprika
2 lb. fillet of flounder

1 c. white wine
2 c. sharp cheddar cheese,
   grated

Brown butter in a shallow baking dish. Salt and pepper fish, then place it in browned butter. Sprinkle fish with paprika. Pour wine over fish and cook in 350° oven for 10 minutes. Remove from oven, baste with sauce, then cover fish with grated cheese. Put this under the broiler until the cheese is melted and crusty (10 minutes). Serve in the sauce. Serves 4.

Skillet Crabmeat

2 c. tarragon vinegar
1-1/2 c. butter

2 tbsp. Worcestershire sauce
4 lb. fresh lump crabmeat

Put all ingredients, except crab, in a saucepan and heat. Add crab. Heat through and serve in chafing dish. Serves 12. A good buffet dish for the "something hot."

Fettuccini Alfredo

2 (8 oz.) pkg. thin egg noodles
1 stick butter

1 c. heavy cream
1 c. Parmesan cheese

Cook noodles according to directions. Drain and return to pot. Add butter and cream and mix well. Add cheese and toss lightly. Spoon into chafing dish or "keep hot" server. Serve with freshly ground pepper. Serves 8. Lovely with green salad and white wine.

Fried Shrimp

1 c. beer (room temp.)
1 c. flour
Pepper to taste

Garlic powder to taste
Salt to taste
Shrimp

Mix all ingredients together. Dip prepared shrimp in mixture and deep fry.

Eye of Round Roast

1 (3-1/2 to 8 lb.) eye of round roast beef or tenderloin

Salt, pepper and lemon-pepper seasoning, to taste

Preheat oven to highest possible setting. Sprinkle roast with salt, pepper, and lemon-pepper. Place on rack in shallow roasting pan. Bake only **four minutes per pound.** Turn off oven; **do not open door.** Leave roast in oven for 1-1/2 to 2 hours. If desired warm, reheat in moderate oven, but be careful not to overcook. (The roast will be pink on the inside.) Serves 8-10.

Pork Chops and Apples

6 pork chops

4 unpeeled apples, cored and sliced

1/4 c. brown sugar

1 tsp. cinnamon

Brown chops on both sides in hot fat. Place apple slices in a greased baking dish. Sprinkle with sugar and cinnamon. Top with pork chops, cover and bake 350° for 1 to 1-1/2 hours. Serves 4-6.

Beef Burgundy

4 lb. beef sirloin, cut into 1-inch cubes

4 pkg. dry onion soup mix

3 (4 oz.) cans of sliced mushrooms

3 c. burgundy wine

Place beef cubes, onion soup mix and wine in a dutch oven. Mix well. Cover and bake at 350° for 3 hours. Stir occasionally. Add mushrooms 15 minutes before cooking time is up. Serve over white or wild rice.

Beef Burgundy II

3 lb. round steak, cut into
small pieces
1 can cream of mushroom soup

1 can beef bouillon soup
3/4 c. red wine
1/2 c. water

Mix together the meat, soups, and red wine. Place in casserole dish uncovered at 350° for about 2-1/2 to 3 hours. The last 1/2 hour add the water. It should be stirred a couple of times while cooking and if it seems too dry, cover with tin foil until done. Serves 6. Serve over medium size noodles.

Pot Roast in Wine Sauce

4 lb. roast (shoulder or chuck)
Salt and pepper
1 clove garlic

1 c. red wine (burgundy)
1 pkg. dry onion soup
1 or 2 c. water

Salt and pepper and insert garlic in center of roast. Put in roaster and brown uncovered at 400°. Pour wine over roast, cover and continue to roast at 325°, basting every half hour. Cook about 45 minutes per pound or until tender. Last 30 minutes sprinkle onion soup over roast and add water, mixing well and basting with other juices. Cover and cook until done. May use gravy as is or add a little cornstarch.

Mock Beef Wellington

4 (6 oz.) pieces of beef
tenderloin
Butter

Chopped fresh mushrooms
4 Pepperidge Farm patty shells

Defrost patty shells. Brown meat on both sides. Saute mushrooms in butter. Roll out patty shells. Place piece of tenderloin on pastry, and mushrooms on meat and wrap pastry around meat. Bake at 425° for 18 to 20 minutes. Serves 4.

Horseradish Steak

1-1/4 lb. boneless round steak
1/2 tsp. salt
1/4 c. vegetable oil
1/4 c. prepared horseradish

1/2 c. all-purpose flour
1/2 tsp. pepper
1 c. water

Trim excess fat from steak; cut into serving-size pieces. Combine flour, salt, and pepper. Dredge steak in flour mixture. Brown in hot oil; add water. Top each piece of steak with horseradish; cover, reduce heat, and simmer 45 minutes or until tender. Yield: 4 servings.

Fried Catfish

6 sm. catfish, cleaned and
    dressed
2 c. self-rising cornmeal

1 tsp. salt
1/4 tsp. pepper
Oil

Sprinkle catfish with salt and pepper. Place cornmeal in paper bag. Drop catfish in bag, one at a time; shake until coated. Fry in deep hot oil (375°) until golden brown; drain well. Serves 4.

Oriental Grilled Chops

8 pork chops (thick cut)
1/2 c. lemon juice
1/2 tsp. garlic salt

1/2 c. soy sauce
2 tbsp. ground ginger or
    4 tbsp. grated fresh ginger

Place chops in shallow pan in single layer. Mix remaining ingredients; pour over chops. Marinate, covered, in refrigerator overnight; turn once or twice. Cook on hot charcoal grill until done. Baste occasionally with marinade. Chops may be baked in marinade in 350° oven for 1 to 1-1/4 hours. **MICRONOTE:** Preheat browning skillet 4-1/2 minutes on HIGH. Drain chops. Place in skillet to sear on both sides. Cook on HIGH for 5 minutes. Reduce power to MEDIUM; cook 10-12 minutes. Turn dish several times during cooking. Serves 8.

Chili

1 lb. ground beef	2 tsp. chili powder
1 sm. onion, chopped	1 c. water
2 tsp. Wesson oil	

Mix all ingredients in boiler or pan and cook approximately 1 hour. Add water as necessary. Salt and pepper to taste. Delicious on hot dogs and hamburgers.

Gourmet Trout

12 sm. trout	Dijon mustard
Salt and lemon-pepper to taste	1/2 c. butter (no substitution)
Lemon wedges	

Rub inside of trout with mustard; sprinkle inside with salt and lemon-pepper. Heat skillet to medium. Add butter to melt. Fry trout in butter 4 minutes on each side. Flake with fork to test for doneness; do not overcook. Serve with lemon wedges. **TO BAKE:** Line shallow baking pan with aluminum foil. Prepare trout as above. Place in pan in single layer. Add milk to 1/4-inch depth around trout. Bake at 350° for 20 minutes, until fish flakes easily. **MICRONOTE:** Rub inside of trout with mustard; do not salt until end of cooking period. Cover with plastic wrap; vent. Cook on HIGH 6-8 minutes or until fish flakes easily; turn dish several times while cooking. Serves 6.

Pork Chops

4 pork chops	1/2 c. catsup
4 tbsp. water	2 tbsp. brown sugar
4 lemon slices	

Brown chops on both sides in skillet. Pour off grease. Mix catsup, brown sugar, and water. Place 1 lemon slice on each chop; pour catsup mixture over chops. Simmer, covered, 30 minutes or until tender. **MICRONOTE:** Preheat browning skillet 4-1/2 minutes. Add chops; brown on both sides. Pour off grease. Mix catsup, sugar and water. Place lemon slice on each chop. Pour catsup mixture over chops. Cover; cook on HIGH 15-20 minutes depending on thickness of chops. Serves 4.

Standing Rib Roast

1 (4 to 6 lb.) rib roast
Pepper
Worcestershire (optional)
Salt
1 c. water (optional)

Salt and pepper roast. Place meat on trivet in open pan with fat side up. Bake at 325°:
    25 minutes per pound for rare roast
    30 minutes per pound for medium roast
    35 minutes per pound for well-done roast
Remove to platter; slice. If gravy is desired, pour off some grease from roasting pan. Add water, Worcestershire, salt, and pepper to taste to remaining drippings. Heat through. Pass with roast. Serves 8-10.

Mexican Casserole

1 lb. hamburger, browned and
    drained
1 can Spanish rice
1 (8 oz.) can tomato sauce
Sharp cheese

Mix, put half in casserole, cover with layer of cheese, pour in remainder and cover with additional cheese. Bake at 350° until bubbly and slightly browned.

Fried Oysters

1 (12 oz.) container of fresh,
    select oysters, drained
1-1/2 c. corn meal
Vegetable oil
1/4 tsp. salt
1/8 tsp. pepper
2 eggs, beaten

Combine dry ingredients in a medium size bowl. Dip oysters in eggs. Dredge oysters in meal and fry in deep, hot oil, at least 375°, 1-1/2 minutes or until golden brown, turning once. Drain on paper towel; serve immediately. Four servings.

Oyster Pie

2 c. sweet milk
1 qt. of fresh oysters
Approximately 24 saltine
   crackers

1 tsp. salt
1/2 tsp. pepper
1 stick butter

Grease a 3-quart baking dish with butter. Alternate layers of cracker crumbs and oysters dotted with butter. Begin with crackers and end with crackers topped with butter. Over this, pour milk so that the contents are barely covered. You may add the salt and pepper to the milk. Refrigerate for several hours. Bake about 1 hour at 350°. Serve immediately. Serves about 10 people.

Baked Hen

1 (5 lb.) baking hen
1 orange, quartered
1 lb. fresh mushrooms

Salt and pepper
1 pt. half-and-half, divided

Wipe hen with damp cloth. Rub inside and out with salt and pepper. Place orange quarters in cavity. Place in baking dish slightly larger than hen. Bake at 425° for 20 minutes. Reduce heat to 350°. Pour 1 cup half-and-half over hen. Bake at 350° for 10 minutes. Pour remaining half-and-half over hen. Bake at 350° for 1 hour. Place mushrooms around hen; stir to coat with juices. Place tent of foil over hen; bake 15 minutes more. Garnish with parsley to serve. (Same method can be used for turkey breast or whole broiler-fryer, increasing or decreasing baking time according to size of fowl.) Serves 6-8.

Grilled Pork Chops

4 (3/4- to 1-in. thick) pork chops
3/4 tsp. lemon-pepper seasoning

1/4 tsp. salt
1/2 tsp. dried whole oregano

Sprinkle pork chops with salt, lemon-pepper and oregano. Place chops 4 to 5 inches from coals. Grill over low to medium-hot coals 25 minutes or until the chops are no longer pink, turning once. Yield: 4 servings.

Pork Chops and Sauerkraut

4 (1/2-in. thick) pork chops
1 (14 oz.) can sauerkraut with
   caraway seeds
1 tbsp. vegetable oil
1 lg. tomato, peeled and
   cubed

Brown chops on both sides in hot oil in a heavy skillet. Top with sauerkraut and tomato. Cover and simmer 40 minutes or until chops are tender. Yield: 4 servings.

Ham and Red-Eye Gravy

2 (1/2-in. thick) ham steaks
   (about 1 lb. each)
1 c. strong black coffee
1-1/2 c. milk
2 tbsp. vegetable oil, divided
1/4 tsp. pepper

Place ham in a large shallow container; pour milk over ham. Cover and refrigerate 8 hours. Remove ham from milk. Cut slashes in fat to keep ham from curling. Cook 1 slice of ham in 1 tablespoon oil in a heavy skillet over low heat until light brown, turning once. Remove from skillet, and keep warm. Drain off pan drippings, reserving for gravy. Repeat procedure with remaining oil and ham. Add pan drippings, coffee, and pepper to skillet; bring to a boil, stirring constantly. Reduce heat, and simmer 3 minutes. Serve gravy with ham and hot biscuits. Yield: 4 servings.

Broiled Flounder

2 tbsp. butter or margarine,
   melted
Lemon wedges
4 (4 to 6 oz.) flounder fillets
2 tsp. Fish-and-Seafood
   Seasoning Blend

Line a shallow baking pan with aluminum foil; lightly brush foil with a small amount of butter. Arrange fillets in prepared pan. Brush fillets with remaining butter, and sprinkle with Fish-and-Seafood Seasoning Blend. Broil 5 inches from heat 10 minutes or until fish flakes easily when tested with a fork. Garnish flounder fillets with lemon wedges. Yield: 4 servings.

Desserts

Peach Cobbler

1 can sliced peaches (lg.)
1 lg. box peach Jell-O (6 oz.)
1 box yellow cake mix

1 stick margarine
1-1/2 c. cold water

Place peaches in a large pan, juice and all. Sprinkle Jell-O over peaches. Sprinkle cake mix over Jell-O and peaches. Cut margarine in small slices and place over cake mix. Pour water over all layers — do not stir or mix layers. Bake 350° for 1 hour.

Graham Cracker Delight

2 sticks butter
1/2 c. sugar
1 c. chopped nuts

Graham crackers (Saltines can be used)

Cover jelly roll pan with foil. Break graham crackers apart and place as close as possible without overlapping. Boil the butter and sugar for 3 minutes, add nuts, and spread over crackers. Preheat oven 350° and bake for 10 minutes. Let cool and break apart again.

Oatmeal Shortbreads

1 c. butter
2/3 c. brown sugar, packed

1-1/2 c. plain flour
2/3 c. rolled oats, uncooked

Blend together butter and sugar. Add flour gradually. Stir in oats. Spread batter into a greased 15 x 10 x 1-inch pan. Use knife to make a thin layer covering the pan. Bake at 350° for approximately 30 minutes. Cut while hot and let cool in pan on rack.

Pulled Mints

1 c. water
4 tbsp. butter
1 lb. or 2 full c. sugar

6 drops oil of peppermint
1/2 tsp. food coloring

Bring water to a boil and add butter. Gradually add sugar and stir until dissolved. Cook rapidly until it spins a thread (261°). Remove from heat and pour on buttered marble slab. Add peppermint and coloring. As soon as candy stiffens around edges, fold to center and pull. Pull until pliable but not stiff. Cut into desired size mints with scissors. Store in tins to cream with waxed paper between layers.

Spiced Nuts

1 c. sugar
2 tsp. ground cinnamon
1/2 tsp. salt

1/4 c. water
2 c. pecan halves

Cook sugar, cinnamon, salt and water until it spins a thread or about 5 minutes from the time it begins to boil. Stir in nuts quickly and pour out on a buttered platter. Cool. Break into pieces.

Mama's Caramel Fudge

3 c. white sugar, divided
2/3 c. milk

1 c. nuts, chopped
2 tbsp. butter

Cook 2 cups sugar, milk and butter to a soft boil (234-238°); remove from heat but keep warm. Brown remaining 1 cup of sugar in a heavy frying pan, being careful not to burn sugar. When sugar is melted and lightly browned, pour slowly into cooked mixture stirring constantly. Add nuts, and stir until the fudge begins to get firm. Pour into well-buttered 8 x 12-inch pan, cool and cut into squares. Makes 36 pieces.

Peanut Butter Crisps

1/3 c. peanut butter
1/3 c. cooking oil

Pinch of salt
8 slices of bread

Trim bread and save crusts. Cut into strips 1/2 x 1/4. Place bread strips and crusts in oven and bake at 200° for 1 hour. Dip toasted strips in peanut butter, oil and salt mixture, then in finely crushed bread crumbs made from toasted crusts. Store in airtight container and they will keep crisp forever.

Cranberry Sherbet

1 tbsp. gelatin
1/2 c. cold water
4 c. cranberries

2 c. sugar
2/3 c. orange juice
2-1/2 c. water

Turn refrigerator to coldest setting. Sprinkle gelatin over 1/2 cup cold water to soften. Cook cranberries in 2-1/2 cups water, covered, until skins pop open. Force through colander or sieve. Add sugar and gelatin mixture and heat until dissolved. Cool. Add orange juice. Turn into two ice trays (without dividers). Freeze until firm. Take out of trays and beat mixture until thick and mushy. Return to trays and freeze. Especially good with turkey dinners at Thanksgiving and Christmas.

Banana Whip

4 bananas
1 c. whipping cream

1/4 c. sugar
1 tsp. lemon juice

Cut up bananas and blend until smooth. Whip cream until stiff, adding sugar and lemon juice. Fold into bananas. Pour into sherbert dishes and refrigerate for two hours. Garnish with mint leaves or lemon peel. Serves 6.

Chocolate Mousse

4 lg. eggs, separated
6 oz. semi-sweet chips

1/2 c. whipping cream
2 tbsp. sugar

Beat egg yolks slightly with fork. Melt chocolate chips over hot water. Add egg yolks to chocolate chips. Beat egg whites until foamy. Add sugar and beat whites until stiff. Carefully fold egg whites into chocolate mixture. Spoon into 1 large bowl or six small compotes. Chill several hours. Top with whipped cream, crushed almonds or grated chocolate. Serves 6.

Mocha Mousse

1/2 pt. whipping cream
1-1/2 tsp. instant coffee

1 tsp. cocoa
1/2 c. confectioners sugar

Whip ingredients together until thick. Serve in pot de cremes or demitasse cups. Serves 6-8.

Melon Ball Compote

1-1/2 c. watermelon balls
1-1/2 c. cantaloupe balls

Lemon slices
1-1/2 c. honeydew melon balls

Mix all fruits together. Serve in chilled glasses. Add slices of lemon and mint sprigs, before serving.

Homemade Ice Cream

2 c. milk
2 c. sweetened fruit (crushed
  pineapple, strawberries,
  peaches or any other kind)

1 c. sour cream
1 can Eagle Brand milk
  (sweetened condensed)

Mix ingredients together well. Pour into freezer container of ice cream churn. Churn until frozen.

Roasted Pecans

4 c. pecan halves
Salt

1/2 c. melted butter

Coat pecans with butter. Place in shallow roasting pan. Bake at 300° for 30-40 minutes, stirring occasionally. Drain on absorbent toweling. Salt to taste. Cool. Store in airtight container. Yield: 4 cups.

Strawberries Elegante

2 c. strawberries
2 c. plain yogurt

6 tbsp. brown sugar
2 tsp. vanilla

Mix together the ingredients and chill. Serves 8.

Vanilla Ice Cream

2 (14 oz.) cans sweetened
   condensed milk

1 qt. half-and-half
1 tbsp. + 1 tsp. vanilla extract

Combine all ingredients, mixing well. Pour ice cream mixture into freezer can of a 1-gallon hand-turned or electric freezer. Freeze according to manufacturer's instructions. Ripen ice cream 1 hour, if desired. Yield: 2-1/2 quarts.

Caramel Surprise

1 qt. vanilla ice cream
1/4 c. + 2 tbsp. Kahlua or
   other coffee-flavored
   liqueur

4 (1-1/8 oz.) English toffee-
   flavored candy bars, frozen
   and crushed

Spoon alternate layers of ice cream and crushed candy into 6 parfait glasses. Top each with 1 tablespoon Kahlua. Yield: 6 servings.

Chocolate Dipped Strawberries

1 lge. pkg. chocolate chips
1/4 c. vegetable oil

Firm, fresh strawberries or
sliced bananas

Melt chocolate chips and oil over hot, not boiling, water. Stir until smooth. Remove from heat, but leave over hot water. Dip fruit; place on foil-lined cookie sheet. Chill in refrigerator for 10 minutes.

Black Forest Torte

1 (18-1/4 oz.) pkg. devil's
    food cake mix with pudding
1 (21-oz.) can cherry pie filling

1 (8 oz.) container frozen
    whipped topping, thawed

Prepare cake mix according to package directions. Spoon batter into a greased and floured 10-inch tube pan; bake according to package directions. Cool in pan 10 minutes; remove from pan, and let cool completely on a wire rack. Slice cake horizontally to make 3 layers. Place bottom layer on cake platter; spread with about 1 cup whipped topping, and top with one-third of cherry pie filling. Repeat process with second and third layers. Chill well. Yield: one 10-inch cake.

Melon Balls

1-1/2 c. cantaloupe balls
1/4 c. amaretto

1-1/2 c. honeydew melon balls
1/2 c. slivered almonds, toasted

Combine first 3 ingredients; toss gently to coat. Chill 1 hour. Spoon into individual compotes; sprinkle with almonds, and serve immediately. Yield: 4 servings.

Pineapple Slush

1 (5-1/4 oz.) can pineapple
    tidbits, undrained
2 c. pineapple sherbet

1 med. banana, chilled
1/4 c. milk

Combine all ingredients in container of an electric blender; process until mixture is smooth. Yield: 3 cups.

Boiled Custard

1-1/2 qt. whole milk
1-1/2 tsp. vanilla or brandy
    flavoring

1-1/2 c. sugar
8 egg yolks

Scald the milk in a double boiler. Beat the yolks until light, then add the sugar. When a skim forms on the milk, slowly pour about 2 cups of the milk into the egg mixture, stirring constantly. Return to the remaining hot milk in the double boiler and cook until the spoon is coated. Stir all the time. Remove from the heat and add flavoring. Do not overcook for the mixture will curdle. I cook so the consistency is such that you drink it from a crystal compote or champagne glass that has been chilled. This is the old time recipe our grandmothers used.

Banana-Berry Flip

1 c. strawberry-flavored
    carbonated beverage
1 c. vanilla ice cream

1 med. size ripe banana,
    quartered

Combine all ingredients in container of an electric blender; process mixture until smooth. Serve immediately. Yield: about 3-1/2 cups.

Green Grapes

1/4 c. firmly packed light
    brown sugar
Mint sprigs (optional)

1/2 c. commercial sour cream
5 c. seedless green grapes,
    washed and stemmed

Combine brown sugar and sour cream in a large mixing bowl. Stir in grapes. Chill several hours. Spoon into individual serving dishes. Garnish with mint, if desired. Yield: 6 to 8 servings.

Sherbet

1/2 gal. mint sherbet
2 boxes Birdseye frozen
  mixed fruit

3/4 c. sweet red sherry

Six hours prior to serving, thaw fruit and mix with sherry. Let stand at room temperature, about 4 hours. Refrigerate approximately 1-1/2 hours prior to serving. Spoon fruit mixture over individual servings of mint sherbet. Serves 10.

Coconut Cake

16 oz. sour cream
2 c. sugar

2 pkg. frozen coconut
1 yellow or white cake mix

The day before you bake the cake, mix together frosting ingredients and let stand in refrigerator overnight. Bake cake mix. Slice the two layers in half making four thin layers. Frost. Keep refrigerated. NOTE: Additional coconut may be sprinkled over top of cake.

Dump Cake

1 can crushed pineapple
  (lg. size)
1 can cherry pie filling

1 box yellow cake mix
1-1/2 sticks butter

Grease 2-inch-deep casserole. Place all ingredients in order given. Bake in oven for one hour at 350°.

Lemon Mousse

1 can evaporated milk
1 c. sugar

1/2 c. lemon juice
1 graham cracker crust

Empty evaporated milk into a small, deep bowl. Place in freezer (uncovered) until crystals form. Remove from freezer. Beat on high speed with electric mixer, gradually adding sugar and lemon juice. Beat until fluffy. Pour over crust; spread flat. Sprinkle lemon rind or graham cracker crumbs on top to decorate. Place in freezer until firm (3-4 hours). Serves 8-10.

Amaretto Cake

1 ready-to-eat Angel Food
    cake (loaf or tube type)
1 lg. carton Cool Whip

Amaretto
1/2 gal. ice cream (any flavor)

Split cake into 3 sections lengthwise. Place first section on cake plate. Drizzle 3 tablespoons Amaretto over cake. Cover with 2 inches of ice cream. Place second section of cake on top of ice cream layer. Drizzle with 3 tablespoons of Amaretto. Cover with 2 inches of ice cream. Place third section of cake on top of ice cream. Drizzle with 3 tablespoons of Amaretto. Fold 3 tablespoons of Amaretto into large carton of Cool Whip. Frost top and sides of cake. Freeze. **NOTE:** Amaretto keeps cake from freezing hard, so you can remove it from freezer and serve immediately. When ready to serve, slice a 1"-1-1/2" thick slice.

Fresh Strawberry Pie

1 (8-in.) pie shell, baked
1 qt. strawberries

3 tbsp. cornstarch
1 c. sugar

Place half of the strawberries in shell. Cook the remaining half with sugar and cornstarch until thick. Pour this mixture over raw strawberries. Put in refrigerator. Serve with whipped cream if desired. Serves 6.

Klondike Dessert

Klondike Bars
Chocolate Sauce

Cool Whip
Cherries

Place chocolate sauce on plate. Place bars on sauce. Put 1 scoop of Cool Whip on top of bar. Drizzle more sauce over Cool Whip. Put cherry on top.

Pineapple Cake

1 (No. 303) can crushed
   pineapple
1 butter pecan cake mix

1 stick margarine or butter
Whipped cream or ice cream

Grease square pan (9 x 9 x 2-inch) with butter. Place crushed pineapple, juice and all, in bottom of pan. Sprinkle the dry cake mix in a layer over the pineapple. Melt the butter and pour over the cake mixture. Bake 45-50 minutes at 350°. Cut into squares and serve warm with either whipped cream or vanilla ice cream. Serves 8. This dessert keeps people guessing what ingredients are used!

Graham Cracker Strawberry Pie

1 (20 oz.) can crushed pineapple
1 (21 oz.) can strawberry pie
   filling

1 sm. can condensed milk
Graham cracker pie shell

Mix all the ingredients, and pour into a graham cracker pie shell. Garnish with Cool Whip to serve.

Lemonade Pie

1 sm. can frozen lemonade, thawed

1 (9 oz.) carton Cool Whip, thawed

1 (15 oz.) can sweetened condensed milk

2 baked 9-in. pie shells

Bake pie shells and let cool. Mix together milk and Cool Whip. Add thawed lemonade. Stir until thick. Spread into cool pie shells. Chill in refrigerator for 3 hours before serving. **NOTE:** 1 cup chopped pecans and 1 small can crushed, drained pineapple can also be added to this same recipe. Add them after the mixture begins to thicken. Pile up mixture in pie shells. Food coloring can be added too. If limeade is used instead of lemonade, it can be colored green and tastes like a Key Lime Pie.

Lemon Chess Pie

1-1/3 c. sugar

Juice and grated rind of 2 lemons

3 eggs

1/2 stick butter or margarine

Mix all ingredients thoroughly and pour into unbaked pie shell. Bake 40-45 minutes at 350°.

Pastry Shells

2 sticks margarine

2 pkg. cream cheese

2 c. plain flour

Cream margarine and cream cheese; add small amounts of flour. Mix well and chill. Roll out small amounts of dough (size of baseball). Leave remaining dough in refrigerator. Roll dough out on floured pastry mat. Roll dough thin (thickness of dough will determine how many dozen shells). Use small ungreased muffin pans to bake shells. Prick bottom of pastry with fork. Bake 350° for 10 minutes or until edge of pastry shell is golden brown. Makes 8-9 dozen. (Shells freeze well — take out of freezer and put into 100° oven until they are warm. Cool before filling.)

Praline Shortbread Cookies

1 c. butter, softened
1-1/2 c. all-purpose flour
1/2 c. ground pecans

3/4 c. firmly packed dark
brown sugar

Cream butter; gradually add brown sugar, beating at medium speed of an electric mixer until light and fluffy. Stir in flour and ground pecans. (Dough will be stiff.) Divide dough into 6 equal portions; pat each portion to a 6-inch circle on lightly greased cookie sheets. Score dough into 8 wedges, using a fluted pastry wheel. Press outside edges of dough with tines of a fork. Bake at 325° for 20 minutes or until cookies are lightly browned. Let cool on cookie sheets; break into wedges. Yield: 4 dozen.

Spiced Shortbread Cookies

1 c. butter or margarine,
softened
2 c. all-purpose flour

2/3 c. sifted powdered sugar
1-1/2 tsp. allspice

Cream butter; gradually add sugar, beating at medium speed of an electric mixer until light and fluffy. Add spice, and beat well. Stir in flour. (Dough will be stiff.) Shape dough into 1-1/4-inch balls, and place 2 inches apart on lightly greased cookie sheets. Lightly press cookies with a floured cookie stamp or fork to flatten to 1/4-inch thickness. Bake at 325° for 15 to 18 minutes or until done. Let cool on wire racks. Yield: 2-1/2 dozen.

Quick Cookies

1 box of any flavor cake mix
(except white)

1 stick margarine, melted
2 eggs

Mix together all ingredients. Drop by teaspoon onto greased cookie sheet. Bake at 350° for 10-12 minutes. The flavor of the cookies can be changed by using a different cake mix.

Lace Cookies

1 stick butter
1 c. brown sugar
1 c. oatmeal

2 tbsp. flour
Pinch of salt

Mix all ingredients and chill. Roll into little balls about the size of a marble. Place on cookie sheet very far apart as they melt down as they cook. Bake at 375° for about 7 minutes. Makes about 4 dozen.

Butter Cookies

1 lb. butter
1 c. sugar
2 eggs

4 c. flour (all-purpose pre-
    sifted)

Cream butter and sugar well by hand. Add eggs and continue creaming until very fluffy. Add flour gradually. (May need a little more flour to reach non-sticky stage.) Use cookie press for desired shapes. Bake on ungreased cookie sheet at 350° until slightly brown. Remove to brown paper to crisp. Makes 80-100 cookies.

Chocolate Oatmeal Cookies

1 pkg. Duncan Hines Brownie
    Mix (regular size)
1/2 c. chopped nuts

1 c. uncooked rolled oats
1/4 c. water
1 egg

Preheat oven to 350°. Empty brownie mix and chocolate flavor packet into medium size bowl. Add all other ingredients and mix well with a spoon. Drop from a teaspoon onto a greased cookie sheet. Bake for 10-12 minutes. Cool on cookie sheet for 1 minute, then remove to rack for cooling.

Overnight Cookies

2 egg whites, at room
    temperature
2/3 c. sugar

1 c. nuts
1 (6 oz.) pkg. chocolate chips

Preheat oven to 350°. Beat egg whites until stiff. Add sugar a little at a time. Fold in nuts and chips. Using teaspoon, spoon on cookie sheet. Put in oven. **Turn oven off.** Do not open until the next morning.

Candy Nuts

1 c. sugar
1/2 tsp. cinnamon
1/4 c. canned milk

2 tsp. water
1-1/2 c. pecan halves

Combine sugar, cinnamon, milk and water. Cook on slow heat until it forms a soft ball. Add pecan halves. Pour out on waxed paper and separate.

Peanut Butter Cups

12 oz. peanut butter
1 box confectioners sugar

1-1/2 sticks melted margarine
1 (6 oz.) pkg. chocolate chips

Mix well peanut butter, sugar and margarine and press into 9 x 12-inch pan; spread melted chocolate chips over this mixture. (You can use large Hershey Bars.) Chill.

English Toffee

1/2 lb. (2 sticks) butter (not
    oleo or margarine)
1 c. crushed or ground pecans

1 c. white sugar
1 (6 oz.) pkg. chocolate chips

Line a 13 x 9 x 2 pan or a cookie sheet with waxed paper. Sprinkle bottom of pan with 1/3 c. of pecans which have been ground coarsely (mixture will not cover all of a cookie sheet so sprinkle nuts over about 2/3 of the sheet). Place butter and sugar in a saucepan over medium high heat. Stir constantly with a wooden spoon until candy reaches the hard crack stage. (If you use a candy thermometer, hard crack is 300°. If you do not have a thermometer, test cooked mixture in cold water for a hard crack.) Mixture will begin to brown. Pour over pecans. Sprinkle chocolate chips over hot mixture and spread evenly. Add remaining 2/3 c. nuts over top. Press into chocolate. Let cool in the refrigerator for 1 to 1-1/2 hours. Break into pieces.

Chocolate-Peanut Butter Candy

3 c. chocolate chips
1-1/2 c. sweetened condensed
    milk

3/4 c. confectioners sugar
3 c. peanut butter

Melt chocolate chips in top of double boiler. Mix with the rest of ingredients. Shape into balls about the size of walnuts. Place on wax paper and chill.

White Chocolate Candy

1 lb. white chocolate

1 c. chopped pecans or almonds

Melt chocolate in top of double boiler until it is completely soft. Stir in nuts. Pour onto waxed paper and spread thin (about 1/4-inch thick). Let cool and break into pieces.

Peanut Butter Candy

1 box confectioners sugar
1 (8 oz.) jar peanut butter
  (crunchy)

7 oz. marshmallow cream
1/2 c. milk

Bring sugar and milk to a boil. Boil for exactly 5 minutes. Remove from heat and add remaining ingredients. Mix together well. Pour in 9 x 9 x 2-inch ungreased pan. Cut in squares when cool.

Baked Peanut Butter Candy

1 c. peanut butter
1 c. granulated sugar

1 egg
1 tsp. vanilla

Heat oven to 350°, mix all ingredients together and shape into small balls. Put on ungreased cookie sheet and cook 10 minutes.

Index